7 Lessons from 7 Layoffs

A Guide

7 Lessons from 7 Layoffs

A Guide

Brenda L. Peterson

Dedication

To my amazing husband, Mike, who has supported me in all the ways through many, many layoffs and pretty much everything else ever.

To my favorite child, Wynn, who is insightful, ridiculously smart, supportive, and an all-around badass.

To my lap kitty, Zippy, who thinks she co-authored this book.

To everyone who has helped me through my career transitions. May this book be a solid starting point for all of the paying it forward I need to do.

Contents

Introduction: And so it begins.

Apparently, I Have a Meeting

It pops up on short notice.

It has an ambiguous title.

The invite specifies no other details.

There have been multiple rounds of layoffs already, including at least a few people yesterday. I thought I was in the clear for at least another month.

I chat online with a coworker with a similar meeting scheduled on his calendar. We speculate wildly on whether it means anything and exchange contact information just in case.

A post from a teammate of mine pops up on LinkedIn.

"This morning, I joined the growing ranks of those who hear the dreaded words, 'Your position has been eliminated.'"

So, former teammate, I guess.

I log into the online meeting and see my boss's face. She pauses and nods as we wait awkwardly.

Yup. This is THAT meeting.

"We'll just give Human Resources another minute to get here," she says, then exhales slowly as her eyes well up. "I'm going to try not to cry."

"Me, too."

The HR rep comes on camera as a silent witness just in case things get ugly. I half listen and try to keep a generically pleasant look on my face as my soon-to-be-former boss goes through her script. I catch the high points of her speech.

"Your position has been eliminated...it's not you, it's us...so sorry...we appreciate all you did...it's just this economy...you'll get a letter..."

I sit silently as I dread breaking the news to my husband.

"Do you have any questions?" she asks as the HR rep continues in silent observation.

"I do not," I said. I knew the drill all too well.

She thanks me, and I thank her. It is sad, but we both know it is just business—a transaction. My salary is part of the answer to a mathematical problem that didn't quite add up.

Six minutes flat.

I exhale and log off my work computer for the last time.

Welcome to layoff number seven.

My Professional Beginnings

According to my mother, at the ripe old age of five, I announced that I was going to college. I don't think I even knew what that meant. I certainly didn't have any idea about the tie between a degree and getting a job. Aside from my fleeting dreams of becoming an actor or comedian, my first actual career assessment occurred during my sophomore year in high school. I remember how weird it felt to take a Scantron fill-in-the-bubble test and have it spit out what I should do for a living for the rest of my life. I also remember being horrified at the prospect of my future career being dictated by a multiple-choice test I took when I was 15 years old.

When the results were in, the two leading career suggestions were high school teacher and funeral director. Growing up in a small farming community, I had limited exposure to what all the jobs were. Farmer, milk hauler, working in a store, police officer, doctor, and teacher were most of the career options I knew existed. Teacher it was, I guess.

When I was finishing high school and starting to think about what came next, I remember my guidance counselor also pushing me toward teaching. I'm sure this was influenced by a projected teacher shortage. Fast forward to me finishing my bachelor's degree in English and Middle/Secondary Education. Soon, I was struggling to find a teaching job, mostly because I was part of the now-flooded market full of my peers who had also been encouraged to become teachers. At that point, I wasn't sure if being a schoolteacher was right for me anyway.

After college and working abroad in London, I spent the spring and summer living with my mom as I figured out my post-college plans. I worked as a substitute teacher and a bartender in my hometown. During the day, I attempted to teach Shakespeare to a classroom of high school freshmen. There, I learned how to manage a group of unruly adult-sized humans who were big, loud, and vastly outnumbered me. At night and on weekends, I served drinks and managed drama at the local country club. There, I learned how to manage a group of intoxicated adults who were big, loud, and vastly outnumbered me. These experiences taught me about building relationships, managing people, and mediating conflict. I also learned that I needed to find a for reals grown-up job.

Moving on Up

I started focusing on roles outside the classroom where I could still use my education and writing skills. I moved to Madison, Wisconsin, and worked briefly for an educational publishing company, then found a job as a software trainer. I learned a lot about technology, leading teams, teaching people, and solving problems. I switched jobs and companies on a regular basis for better titles, higher salaries, and additional learning opportunities.

After my first three training jobs, I worked for a small, scrappy technology company. Now, I would call them an early-stage tech startup focusing on what would become SaaS (Software as a Service). At the time, they were a 50-person company experimenting with ideas that might become hugely successful or might become nothing. Spoiler alert: this was one of the companies that eventually became nothing.

About a year into working there, I received an alert that my student loan payment didn't go through. In a panic, I looked at my bank account and saw that my paycheck had bounced. I went to work early the next morning and impatiently paced outside the business manager's office. When he arrived, I told him about my paycheck. He cited bank issues and wrote me a check from another account. I immediately cashed the check. That day, I started looking for a different job.

My First Experience with Layoffs

A couple of weeks later, before I had even heard of anyone doing layoffs, my boss took me aside to tell me the company was eliminating headcount. He mentioned the "dot com bubble." I still had a job but had to pick which of my two training specialists would lose theirs. Amazingly, I managed to make a compelling argument to keep them both. The next day, that small, scrappy company got a little smaller. A week later, I gave my notice.

A Search for Stability

I traded in that volatile tech company for an established retail business with a larger footprint. I was hired for a newly created position where I would develop career paths for the IS (Information Solutions) department. I started in June of 2001, and while I missed some aspects of startup life, I appreciated working for an organization with a stated mission, company values, and a multi-year strategic plan. Taking this job at this company at this point in time was the right choice for me.

A Swing and a Miss

While I appreciated the stability of the role, and that whole thing where my paychecks didn't bounce, it was not the best fit. I worked for a micromanager who scheduled weekly meetings where she "helped me" organize my calendar. While I was brought in to create a new program, there was internal resistance to changing much of anything. About three months in, I felt like I had made a mistake. I started to evaluate my options.

Then 9/11 happened. The terrorist attacks had people rattled, and one of the effects was lower consumer confidence. This meant the retail-focused business I worked for would soon face big decisions. Within a week, consultants were popping up in meetings to point out ways to "increase efficiencies." One Wednesday morning, I walked into work expecting a day full of not-very-productive meetings and found myself sitting home about an hour later. I no longer had to orchestrate my graceful exit. That decision had been made for me.

Even though it had only been a few short months since I saw my coworkers get laid off, I never thought the same thing could happen to me. I was a strong performer, a problem solver, and someone who got the job done. I always met deadlines and earned accolades for my overachievements. Yet here I was. Jobless.

Layoff Number One

My first layoff was nothing short of surreal. As someone who grew up working on my family's dairy farm, not having any type of paid work felt just plain weird. At that time in my life, I was used to having two or more paying jobs instead of no job at all. In addition, the employment market was a wasteland. I bought a newspaper each Sunday to look for jobs, mailed out a few paper resumes, and started using a new website I'd just heard about called Monster.com. I spent most of that never-ending fall and winter sitting in the new house we had just bought, wondering if I would ever work again. Each week, I applied for the two open jobs I could find within a 50-mile radius that had anything at all to do with training. Cleaning, watching nonstop Law & Order reruns, and leaving the house at least once were the cornerstones of my daily routine.

A New Job

After six months of unemployment, I landed a new job as a training specialist supporting staff at a company's branch offices. I worked with a fun team of people, learned a lot, traveled regularly, and earned a few leadership training certifications. I even used tuition reimbursement to start working on my Master's Degree in Adult Education. After about three years there, I was reporting to a manager who encouraged me to treat her like she was my mother (yikes). I decided it was time to move on and sought a management position with more growth potential.

This job change in 2004 would be the last time I voluntarily left a company for the next 19 years.

An Even Cooler New Job

Next, I worked as a sales training manager for a regional company, supporting their office staff and call center. I managed one trainer and designed innovative learning and development programs. I even traveled to deliver a sales and customer success training program I created.

In retrospect, I now realize there were several telltale signs that the company was not all that stable. After a failed attempt to purchase a competitor, an international player acquired the company. Then, a flurry of activity began, including changes to benefits plans and figuring out how to meld the companies together. Before long, the new president was in the office trying to boost morale. His priority was running taste tests on possible new vendors to improve the coffee quality in the breakrooms. His focus culminated in a multi-day all-company event full of team building and generating excitement about the organization's bright future.

Layoff Number Two

One day, my morning trip to the breakroom for fancy new coffee devolved into an impromptu meeting in the conference room. I felt all stability give way as my job ended abruptly. Since my personal life was doing its best to fall completely apart, I planned on using that job as my anchor while moving through some pretty significant life changes.

Even though I'd been through an unplanned job loss before, being laid off again seemed improbable. Despite all the indicators of trouble, I assumed that my first layoff would be my only layoff. Except here I was again.

With most of the areas of my life in upheaval, I decided to make additional big life changes all at once.

A New Job in a New City

Four months later, I finalized my divorce, moved in tandem with my then-former husband to Minneapolis, enrolled my toddler in a new daycare, and began a wonderful learning and development coach role with a non-profit organization.

For the next eight years, I worked with two intelligent and friendly coworkers as I learned the ins and outs of employee benefits programs. Not only did I get to travel around the country to present at conferences, but I also learned about managing my finances, health insurance implications, financial planning, behavioral health, and making sound personal business decisions. I was excited to be in a role where I could see myself staying long-term.

Layoff Number Three

While in that role, the housing bubble burst and Hurricane Katrina hit, which helped kick off "The Great Recession." My employer did several reorganizations and more than a few layoffs. This included one round of what I have heard called "Good Room, Bad Room." This is where everyone gets an email, but some people report to conference room A and learn they are still employed. The others are directed to conference room B and learn their positions have been eliminated.

When it was my turn, though, I just got a plain old out-of-the-blue "Please join us in the HR conference room" call and a letter with information on how to choose my last day of work before my job ended. I was sad that the job I had no plans to leave was no more.

A Learning Leader Role in a Technology Company

This time, I found a new job in only two months. It was the perfect storm of being in the right place at the right time and knowing the right person. A friend of a friend worked at a software company that happened to be looking for someone to create their online learning program. Due to my layoff, I was available, and my connection introduced me to the hiring manager.

Unlike my previous role, this company was in a constant state of growth and change. In the handful of years I was with this company, I had four direct managers, three desks, and multiple job titles. I loved the fast pace and the culture of innovation.

Layoffs Number Four Through Six

Some people say bad things happen in threes. In this case, I had three jobs in a row that were pretty great, followed by three more layoffs that were not great at all. Each was a fast-paced software company and my tenure with all three ended with my role being eliminated due to company restructuring.

These staffing changes were driven by economic challenges, new company ownership, new leadership, sales numbers, and all the other reasons companies decide to make changes. My tenure ranged from about a year to almost four years. Each role I took was a training leadership role where I set the strategy, built a team, and solved interesting problems by creating and implementing training solutions.

While I loved the excitement of each of those tech companies, I realized that I needed to reevaluate.

The Reevaluation After Layoff Number Six

After having three similar jobs end in the same less-than-ideal way, I was exhausted. I also had a child graduating from high school, a house to sell, and a cross-state move to orchestrate. I needed time to heal and the bandwidth to work through a few significant life transitions. After doing some long-overdue soul searching, I decided to look for an individual contributor position with a bigger and more established company that offered stability and a larger training team. My goal was to have interesting work that leveraged my skills, but where I would also have more bandwidth for other areas of life.

An Individual Contributor Role

After my shortest layoff ever, not quite two months, I landed in a non-management role with a company focused on finance. In this learning consultant role, I worked on a team of five incredible people who were supportive and happy to share information. I loved being in an environment where I could learn new things and collaborate with so many smart people. I also had one of the best bosses I have ever had.

Layoff Number Seven

Unfortunately, my intention of working for a bigger company with more stability didn't turn out as planned. After several rounds of quiet layoffs, I made the new org chart and thought I was safe. Two short weeks later,

I realized that the chart was still in flux. The timing was unexpected, yet the result was not surprising. Layoffs were caused by several intersecting factors, including the company being acquired, economic conditions that drastically changed the business, and a new leadership structure. My efforts to find stability had fallen short.

Career Transition Number Seven Would Be Different

I remember the good old days when I felt bad for my friend Tricia because she had been laid off four times. Now, as I worked through post-layoff career transition number seven, I decided to be even more intentional. I focused on my personal growth and documenting my lessons learned to help others going through similar experiences. Out of that intentionality, The Layoff Lady was born. Through blog articles, presentations for The White Box Club® job search group, and this book, I'm committed to sharing information on layoffs, job transitions, and career resilience.

Is Being Laid Off Seven Times Normal?
(Alternate Title: What is Wrong with You, Brenda?)

That's a fair question. I'm guessing that you don't personally know very many people who have been laid off at all—much less seven times. Despite how the numbers here look, I'm not a total screw-up, terrible at what I do for a living, or the least lucky person ever. If I do say so myself, I am a high achiever who is constantly finding new ways to be even better at what I do, which is helping people learn.

My torrid history of layoffs is not solely about me and my skill set. It's also about the company, industry, state of the world, and my chosen profession.

Seven Factors that Prompt Layoffs

There are seven key factors that may indicate a company is considering layoffs and that your job may be at risk:

- **Economic conditions:** Factors impacting the United States or the world often cause financial ripples. Events like The Great Recession, The Covid-19 Pandemic, and The Housing Bubble bursting changed how money flowed to businesses. When times are tight, layoffs may follow.
- **Company finances:** If companies don't hit their sales numbers or invest in a project that doesn't pay off, reducing the number of people on the payroll is a possibility.
- **New leadership:** Having a new company CEO or department head usually means changes are coming. In some cases, new leaders may replace current staff with "their people" as they make organizational changes.
- **New ownership:** Change is inevitable when a company is acquired or part of a merger. Duplicate departments and job titles are eliminated as the combined organization builds their new normal.
- **Company restructuring:** Companies always try to optimize their operations. They may outsource a team or bring a previously external function in-house. They may revisit job titles and the skills and salaries for each role. This means teams will realign, and reporting structures will change, including changing who has which jobs.
- **Reduced responsibilities:** As an employee, if you used to have a really interesting job, and now you have fewer responsibilities, your position may be ending soon.
- **Company culture:** In some companies, it seems like you can do nearly anything and not manage to get yourself fired. In others, they may be quicker to bring people in and out. The company's overall attitude towards change and retention will dictate the amount of employee churn.

It's Never Just One

Often, it's not just one of those factors but several. For example, I worked for a retail company in 2001, just before 9/11. Based on that terrorist attack on US soil, consumer confidence took a hit and retail companies had much lower sales. In addition, the CEO of that company had just retired, and the parent company was taking a more prominent role in day-to-day business. Post 9/11, the company started to look at their operations and decided to restructure to ensure the right people were in the right roles and making the right amount of money for their contribution. All of these factors led to layoffs and company-wide changes.

My Seven Layoffs and those Seven Factors

Of the seven times I've been laid off, the following reasons were factors:

- Economic conditions: 4
- Company finances: 4
- New leadership: 6
- New ownership: 3
- Company restructuring: 7
- Reduced responsibilities: 3
- Company culture: 2

In addition, my chosen profession and the types of companies I have worked for also make a difference. When companies decide to lay people off, the training function is often one of the first to be eliminated, with marketing not far behind. Furthermore, I've often been the only one of me in an organization or had the highest training role within a company. When my job ended, there was often nowhere else for me to go internally. I've also worked for many small companies or organizations closer to the start-up space. These companies tend to have a lot more change, which may include reorganizing and switching directions. That coupled with some incredible luck, here I am, a seven-time layoff survivor.

Seven Lessons from Seven Layoffs

Through my layoffs and many conversations with others in post-layoff career transition, I have learned seven core lessons that can help you navigate this challenging time:

- **Lesson One: Experience your emotions and manage your mindset.** Right after a layoff, people often act hastily out of sheer unbridled panic. Instead, you must attend to two key tasks right away: feeling your feelings and choosing your career transition mindset. Getting your head on straight before springing into action will prepare you for the challenges ahead.

- **Lesson Two: Keep your mind on your money (and your money on your mind).** Most people work to pay their bills and afford the life they want. Unfortunately, when your job ends, so does your main income stream—and possibly your health insurance, too. Making the right short-term changes can help you weather the storm while also minimizing long-term financial repercussions.

- **Lesson Three: Ask yourself, "What do you want to be next?"** Few people take the time to step back from their work life and think, "Is this really what I want to do?" When you go through an unplanned job change, seize this rare opportunity to revisit your career path. Take time for a little structured soul searching and actively decide what you want both long-term and in your next job.

- **Lesson Four: Shape and share your story.** Finding a new job is all about you telling the story of your career. You get to shape your professional narrative so you can share your compelling story with colleagues and potential employers. Learning to talk about where you've been, your skillset, and where you're going is powerful. Weaving in company needs with who you are professionally will help you communicate your value more effectively.

- **Lesson Five: Help people help you.** It's hard for many of us to ask for help. If there was ever a time to avoid going it alone, this is it. Overall, people genuinely want to help others through trying times. You can assist them by being mindful of what you need and asking just the right person. Letting people help you will make managing the emotional, logistical, and practical aspects of this career transition easier.

- **Lesson Six: Examine your energy to take control of your time.** When it comes to achieving a goal, people often focus on time management. While checking the right items off a task list is valuable, having the energy to do so is often overlooked. Figuring out those right things to do, prioritizing tasks, and factoring in your energy levels will help you sustain your job search momentum for the long haul.
- **Lesson Seven: Assess, adapt, and rise above.** Having a plan for success is critical. It is even better to assess how it is going, adapt when needed, and rise above challenges. By anticipating roadblocks and thinking through possible solutions, you can proactively alter your game plan as needed. Learning as you go will help you build resilience and cultivate successful outcomes.

Using These Lessons Learned

As one of my favorite Nelson Mandela quotes states, "I never lose. I either win, or I learn." In my case, I have learned volumes by going through multiple layoffs. I also did enough winning to find myself gainfully employed again, each time in a role that was the right next step for me. Now, I'm excited to share those lessons with you.

Lesson One: Experience your emotions and manage your mindset.

Welcome Back. And Also Goodbye.

It was my first day in the office in a week. I was excited to tell my big game hunter boss that my husband and I almost hit an elk with our truck outside Yellowstone during our cross-country road trip. As I told my story, he looked uncomfortable, laughed awkwardly, and abruptly declared, "We've got a meeting." I grabbed a notebook and followed him as best I could—my short steps trying to keep up with his long strides.

As we walked across the open office, I saw the VP of my department; he looked away when we met on the stairs. Right then, I realized I was being perp-walked to the HR Director's office. While I had already started looking for a new job outside the company, I definitely didn't expect my morning to go like this.

As my boss hovered uncomfortably in the corner, I sat there, listening to the HR Director explain that my job was over. My mind wandered as she covered the details. I was all at once shocked, apathetic, and just plain mad.

I thought back to my last workweek and filled with anger. It was our customer conference, and I had spent a hectic week leading breakout sessions, staffing a resource table, and mingling with clients. I went above and beyond, expended every bit of extroversion I could muster, and skimped on sleep. I went from essential to expendable over the five business days I was on vacation.

The Importance of Experiencing Your Emotions

Losing your job, even through no fault of your own, will bring on a myriad of feelings. Given how much of your life you spend at work, suddenly not having the same job is a monumental change. Not only do you lose your paycheck and a large part of your identity, but you also lose the stability of your day-to-day routine. Having such a significant life change suddenly thrust upon you is unsettling.

Going through a shift of this magnitude requires some adjustments. Suddenly, your paycheck ending, and the need to find a new source of income are at the top of your priority list. Before you rush to solve those very big, very real problems, just stop. Ensure you don't quickly implement a solution you haven't thought through. Before you are in any state to make big-time grown-up life decisions, you need to process the metric ton of challenging emotions your brain is trying to pretend don't exist.

I'm Fine. Really.

When people ask us how we're doing in passing, most people will respond, "Fine."

In times of trouble, that becomes, "I'm fine. Really."

Even if you can appear calm, in reality, you are pretty far from fine. You may not even know how you feel at that moment. In times of stress, you may just hold it together as long as possible. You may also think how you feel right now is irrelevant because you have work to do—like finding a new job and paying your bills.

While stuffing those feelings down might get you by for a while, a whole lot of feelings are coming—and you'll need to deal with them. Realize that managing your emotions doesn't mean ignoring, denying, or manipulating them. Instead, it starts with acknowledging them and working through each one as it comes.

Know, too, that they won't go away if you don't work through them. Instead, they will rear their ugly little heads at the worst time and come out sideways as frustration, anger, and blame. Not only will that be hard for you and those around you, but it can also negatively impact your job search.

Initial Post-Layoff Emotions

As you work through this change, you may feel alright one moment, angry the next, eerily calm, and then in tears. Processing these ever-changing emotions is healthy and necessary. It can also be exhausting. Here are the main players in the flood of feelings you will experience early on.

Shock

The failed network login, the oddly worded message to your personal email, or the last-minute meeting all come out of nowhere. The experience is surreal as you realize your planned workday has just turned into something entirely different.

Even if there were layoff rumors, sudden leadership changes, or low quarterly sales, it's always a surprise at the time it happens to you. After your job suddenly ends, you'll catch yourself thinking about a meeting you need to schedule, a report you need to finish, or a project completion date. Then you'll remember, "Wait—that's not my job anymore." You'll be reminded that the role that earned you the adoration of your peers a week ago now no longer exists for you. You may feel untethered, lost, and irrelevant.

My Shock

The night before, I had toured a new housing development with my toddler and then-husband—we just didn't tell the real estate agent we were looking for two units. That morning, as I filled my coffee cup, I mentally crunched numbers, trying to figure out if I could afford a condo on my own. Soon, a coworker invited me to an impromptu meeting, and I found myself in a conference room with two executives giving me the bad news. Packing up my desk was a blur. Later, I found myself sitting in my car, dumbfounded, trying to make sense of what had just happened.

Anger

You might resent your boss for not fighting for your job. You might be enraged at company leadership for mismanaging the business. You may be irate that you were laid off right before a holiday. You might be livid to have your position eliminated right after a fantastic performance review. You may also be resentful that yesterday's mission-critical work-all-night project has suddenly become unnecessary. You may be bitter about being out of the job instead of that awful coworker or boss. Even if you were planning your exit, you might be upset that you could not leave that job on your terms and timeline.

My Anger

I was searching as quickly as possible to find an answer to an obscure customer question when I was asked to stop by the conference room. I didn't think anything of it—until I was in the room and realized it was me and two HR people. I learned my position was being eliminated and that I'd be sent home for the day. I'd then come back the following day to figure out the details of my exit.

Later that afternoon, a coworker forwarded me a message she had received from my soon-to-be-ex boss. She announced that there were upcoming changes and that my role was being eliminated so the company could hire "some professional trainers." I was furious. My years of work experience, company awards, consistent performance on complex projects, and master's degree in Adult Education somehow didn't make me enough of a "professional trainer" for them. I continued working there for the next month or so to finish my projects. Being in that office—where I apparently was not skilled enough to continue—was a constant source of aggravation.

Sadness

Exiting a job abruptly leaves a big hole in your life, starting with the nine-plus hours per workday being replaced with dead air and uncertainty. The consistency of a morning routine, daily commute, and regularly scheduled meetings are replaced with the dread of not knowing whether your jobless state will last a week or a year. Sometimes, it's easy for you to be hopeful about the future, and other times, it's hard not to be mired in sadness about everything you can't control.

Then there are the relationship changes. People who earlier that day were coworkers, casual friends, or confidants now may be nothing at all to you since you no longer share a workplace. People who played a role in your life—like the helpdesk guy who got his coffee at the same time as you, the lady from accounting with the twins, and the goth twenty-something in your morning meeting—are now gone. You may never interact with them again as you realize some people were just work friends. Others may even avoid you as they try to distance themselves from your jobless state. Still others may go silent because they don't know what to say.

My Sadness

I was so grateful that my job was the one constant in my life. After a week-long all-staff meeting, I was excited about the company's direction and the role I thought I would play in that future. When my job suddenly ended, the source of stability I depended on was gone. Those work relationships, especially with my closest coworkers, changed significantly. Losing that anchor was heartbreaking and made me feel lost as I navigated the most challenging period of change in my life.

Fear

There is plenty to be afraid of in this process. The idea of not having a consistent paycheck is horrifying. Not knowing how long your severance check has to last is unnerving. Wondering how long this period of joblessness will last and what role you'll end up with is, at times, unbearable.

You may ask yourself, "Can I even say I'm a project manager if a company doesn't give me that title?" You'll doubt your abilities and worry that maybe you're not as good at your chosen profession as you thought. You'll despair as you fear that no one else will believe you are good enough to have that job title ever again.

You might worry about being unemployed endlessly and unable to support yourself. You may fear settling for too little by taking the first job offered to you. You may also fear that you are holding out for the "perfect" job offer that may never come. You may be scared to death at the thought of having to do a resume—especially after not even considering changing jobs for years. You might also be nervous that you'll never get a job as good as the one you just had. You may fear getting stuck in a position even worse than your worst job to date. On your least hopeful days, your fear may grow into catastrophizing. You might panic about losing your relationships, reputation, home, and everything that matters to you.

My Fear

After being laid off from a few all-consuming jobs in a row, I needed a break. I was happy when I accepted a less demanding position with a larger company that I thought would be more stable. Soon, a reorganization was underway due to a recent merger, and the quiet layoffs began.

A week later, when that last-minute meeting popped up on my calendar, I feared that was it. Now, I was facing my fourth layoff in five years. At a glance, my resume looked like I couldn't stick with an employer. My most recent job title looked like a huge step backward, and now my career path required an explanation. I worried I'd struggle to get a new job in a highly competitive job market. I dreaded yet another job search and trying to convince people that I was worth hiring.

Like an Idiot

Once you know how the story ends, it's easy to look at the signs and think to yourself—oh, that's what that was all about.

You'll remember that the company canceled two of your projects. Or that you were asked to make a list of all of your work commitments. Or that every layer of leadership above your boss had turned over in the last six months. Or that hiring had essentially stopped. Or that your department was restructuring yet again.

Remember that while each of those events happened, they were alongside many other factors that didn't mean anything in particular. Companies also make decisions using information that many employees won't know about.

My Idiocy

When I started in my position, I was leading training projects and designing new learning programs. Over time, my manager changed four times, the whole company reorganized, and a new leadership team made even more adjustments.

Soon, departments stopped including me in their planning meetings. Eventually, my primary responsibilities could barely be called projects. Given my scaled-back role, I was now vastly overpaid for what was left of my job. I was so busy trying to make the best of a bad situation that I completely missed the writing on the wall.

Relief

The strange benefit of finally being laid off is that you don't have to worry if it's going to happen anymore. Now, you're not apprehensive about finishing a near-impossible project, cranky about a time-wasting meeting, or dreading one more humorless "happy hour" with unpleasant coworkers.

At that moment, you breathe a sigh of relief. You also realize it's not as bad as you imagined. Now, what there is to do is pick yourself up, dust yourself off, and figure out what is next.

My Relief

I was managing a team in a hectic work environment. The workload was unyielding, my team was overextended, and the problems kept piling up.

My new boss demanded explanations for the shortcomings she saw. While I tactfully tried to explain that the results were due to my past manager's decisions, she didn't want to hear it. Soon, she brought in a consultant to "help" me and directed me to copy her and the new consultant on all communications.

I knew I needed an exit strategy, but I was so burned out that I didn't have the energy to make it happen. I remember thinking, "If they would just lay me off, I could find something new." At that moment, I understood what true hopelessness felt like. A few days later, while I was surprised when I realized I was in **that** meeting, I was ultimately relieved because I was free.

Ongoing Career Transition Emotions

Unfortunately, the bad feelings don't happen all at once, so you can feel them quickly and be done. Instead, the feelings come when they come, and you have to deal with them whenever they resurface. Those emotions may look like this:

- You may feel anger each time you see your former employer's name in the news celebrating their accomplishments.
- You may feel sad when you realize you and your household don't get to go to the company picnic or be part of the holiday party this year.
- You may feel fear whenever you read news about more layoffs. You may worry about other job seekers competing for jobs that interest you. You worry about being able to pay your bills as your layoff drags on.

- You may feel shame each time someone asks about your job, and you have to tell them that you are not working because you were just laid off. You may also feel bad about yourself when someone talks about spending money in a way you can't afford right now.

Those same emotions that showed up right away may continue to come and go throughout your career transition. Remember to feel your feelings and work through each emotion in turn. As a very wise nurse midwife once told me, the only way out is through.

Rejection and Negative Emotions

Being jobless post-layoff and searching for a new role is a rough process riddled with rejection. It starts with your former employer kicking you out of the whole company and essentially saying, "You are no longer one of us." At every step of the way, you'll experience people telling you no in a variety of ways. Here is how that rejection may look:

Applying for a job and:

- Hearing the booming emptiness of no reply at all.
- Receiving a rejection email in what feels like mere moments after hitting submit.
- Seeing that role repeatedly reposted as if to say, "We can't find anyone, but certainly not you."

Having what felt like a great interview for a job and:

- Hearing a fat lot of nothing back. Ever.
- Finding out the job is on hold, they made an internal hire, or they went with another candidate.
- Receiving a canned "thanks, but no thanks" email months after your last conversation.

Receiving a job offer and:

- Seeing that the pay rate is significantly below the salary range you had discussed.
- Receiving an offer (after a long delay) with the demand that you accept this instant and start immediately.
- Letting another company know you have an offer and hearing that they do not want to move forward with you as a candidate.

Accepting a job offer and:

- Hearing nothing from your new employer about the details of your first week.
- Getting a last-minute call from the recruiter that your start date has been postponed.
- Having the offer rescinded due to company changes.

My Rejection

It was the last week in November, and I was waiting to hear back about a job. On the day before Thanksgiving, I finished the final step of an excruciating interview process. During that four-hour in-person interview, I completed a sample workday, including meeting with a client, leading a team update, and working on yet another project. I had already endured nine interviews and was convinced I would receive a job offer after this final step.

When I got the call, my point of contact coldly informed me that the company had decided not to proceed with my application. As a lackluster consolation prize, he asked if I would like to be added to their consultant database for possible contract work. I was crushed.

Strategies for Experiencing Your Emotions

Since pretending everything is fine is not a viable long-term strategy, let's look at a few ways to experience those challenging emotions.

Separate the Work Streams

If you have ever been part of a project team, you may be familiar with the idea of work streams. This is a way to group and divide tasks so different teams can complete them. This division of labor helps the team contribute to achieving an overarching goal. For example, if a software company plans to release a new product, one team would develop the software while a separate team would market it to customers. Each of these groups of tasks is a work stream.

After a layoff, you have two distinct work streams that should be managed separately. One work stream is processing your emotions. A separate work stream is searching for new paid work. Both are equally necessary and must be addressed for you to achieve your goals. By dividing up what you need to do and addressing each functional area, you can give each area the attention it needs while keeping them from sabotaging one another. Completing these work streams well will contribute to your goal of getting new paid work.

Acknowledge Each Emotion

There is great power in naming and acknowledging each emotion you experience. Don't pretend that you don't feel how you do. Instead, articulate how you feel at a given point in time. You may use words like these to express what you are feeling:

- I feel scared that I will not be able to make my house payment.
- I feel angry that I won't get my year-end bonus.
- I feel sad that the job that I really liked just ended.

Stating "I feel" a given emotion instead of "I am" that same emotion enables you to acknowledge how you feel while also indicating that the emotion is not the totality of who you are. Saying these statements out loud gets the feeling out of your head and helps you move past it. Doing this exercise regularly will help you process emotions more quickly.

Wallow a Little

It's impossible to will yourself into feeling better. Sometimes, you need to just sit with an uncomfortable feeling for a while and let it run its course. Cry a little. Rewatch your favorite movie for the bijillionth time. Have a little ice cream. Do a puzzle. Take a walk. Take the afternoon off from your to-do list. Although it can be unpleasant, you'll navigate the feeling more quickly if you work through it rather than trying to pretend it's not happening to you.

Research the Problem

If you're worried about something, researching answers and managing your expectations often helps. Having a greater understanding of your challenge and what others have experienced can remove some of the uncertainty.

When I was getting ready to sell my house a few years ago, not knowing how long it would take made me very anxious. After stressing about the uncertainty, I sought answers from other people's experiences. I learned from multiple sources that after 15-20 people tour your home, you are likely to get at least one offer. Having valuable data and understanding what positive action I could take helped me move from idle fear to problem-solving.

When it comes to your job search, consider researching questions like these:

- How many job applications does it typically take to get an interview?
- How long does it take most people to find a new role post-layoff?
- Which companies are hiring?
- What are the current job titles in my field I should target?

Gathering additional information can help you feel more in control while giving you a greater understanding of your challenge and how to work towards your goals.

Take a Social Media Break

Social media, specifically LinkedIn, can be a great job search tool. Conversely, it can also give you the illusion that everyone else is doing great and you are downright hopeless. Posts like "It only took me a week to find my dream job!" or "I'm still employed but I feel SO BAD for my former coworkers who are jobless." or "Every company ever is doing more layoffs!" will only make you feel worse. Remind yourself that social media isn't real life and disengage.

Leverage Basic Self-Care

When everything feels hard, taking care of yourself needs to be one of your top priorities. Here are a few quick and easy ideas to make you feel almost instantly better:

- Take deep breaths.
- Drink water.
- Eat regularly.
- Rest.
- Shower.
- Take a break.
- Go outside.

It's amazing how the small act of taking basic care of yourself makes such a difference. Sometimes, it is as easy as closing your eyes and taking a moment of silence before you move on. Contrary to what some might say, you're not being lazy or undisciplined. You're being human and ensuring you can sustain the effort and energy needed to navigate this significant life transition.

Manage Those Unhelpful Thoughts

Along with those emotions come a series of unhelpful thoughts you may have intermittently throughout your career transition. Here are a few of my greatest hits:

- I will never work again.
- I am not really that good at what I do.
- Everyone else is getting a job in no time, and I'm a big loser.
- The job I will be forced to settle for will be worse than my worst job.

These thoughts will come and go. Be sure to remind yourself that thinking a given thought does not make it true. Acknowledge them as they go by, realize they result from those ongoing emotions, and let them go.

The Importance of Managing Your Mindset

Your mindset is your overall approach to dealing with the world. It includes how you think about your current situation, including your assumptions about what is true. Getting your head right will help you manage all the parts of your job search, including the ups and downs of looking for new paid work.

When people search for a new role, successful people believe that the future will be good. They also acknowledge that there will be challenges to overcome along the way. When it comes to mindset, optimists believe everything will be great, realists see things as they truly are, and pessimists believe everything will be terrible. I have found that being a Realistic Optimist is the optimal mindset for job search success.

Be a Realistic Optimist

When you're in a career transition, being aware of the fundamental challenges of job searching and staying hopeful about the future is an excellent way to deal with the struggles inherent in the process.

First off, you need to be realistic. This includes being aware of the possible pitfalls, learning more about challenges, and addressing each issue as it arises. It does not mean pretending things are not the way they are or over-focusing on factors you can't control. It's about acknowledging what is and adjusting your actions and expectations accordingly. In addition to being realistic, it's also valuable to be optimistic. For example, while acknowledging the situation as it is, you are also keeping your spirits up and expecting good things to happen.

As a Realistic Optimist, you can acknowledge that things won't always go your way but that it doesn't mean the world is against you. When you commit to doing the right things and staying the course, you'll have a better experience overall and position yourself for a positive outcome.

The Realistic Part: Acknowledging Job Search Realities

Understanding and acknowledging core truths about the job search process is a great place to start. It's also helpful to remind yourself that these factors make job searching hard for everyone. These realities include the following:

- The hiring process at a company can be anywhere from organized to chaotic.
- Hiring will rarely be the highest priority for the people interviewing you.
- Some companies do not communicate well during the hiring process.
- Job titles may mean different things at different companies.
- Job titles and job descriptions may be vague, inaccurate, outdated, or overly ambitious.
- Hiring managers and recruiters may not know what they want from a given role.
- You may not get an interview for a job regardless of your qualifications.
- Working time passes more quickly than unemployed job seeker time.
- Not every potential employer will offer you a job or a salary that aligns with your goals.
- You will hear significantly more "no" than "yes."

The Optimist Part: Your General Outlook

Take on a mindset that helps you contextualize these challenges and note your progress, not just your pitfalls. These statements are affirmations that resonate with me:

- I will commit to doing the right things consistently to help me get a new job.
- Finding the right job for me might take a while.
- I only need one job.
- I will do my research and put my work in so I'm prepared when opportunities arise.
- I will commit to doing the right things consistently during my job search.
- My core responsibility is to demonstrate my value.
- I will assume a positive intent from others I encounter.
- I will make the right business decisions for me.

You Are The CEO of You

I often remind people that layoffs are just business. At its most basic level, an organization makes a reduction in force to help position them for future success. Since salaries are often a company's biggest expense, when budgets get tight, some companies eliminate jobs.

Unfortunately, the same organizations that may preach the values of hard work and loyalty to the company may also show that they care about you very little when the numbers don't add up.

I think it's time to change how you think about your life, your value, and your relationship with work.

Remind yourself that you are not just a unit of productivity beholden to an employer. In reality, your career is your business, and you are the CEO of You. Just like the executive team at a company needs to make tough decisions for the organization's greater good, you need to make business decisions that are in the best interests of you and your household.

As the CEO of You, it's time to think about what success looks like for your business. What are your assets? What are your marketable skills? Which company or companies should be your business partners? When is it time for you to end a business relationship that is no longer mutually beneficial? When is it time for you to pursue a new opportunity that is better aligned with your life?

Making decisions as the CEO of You will change your life. Now, you are not an employee who has to do whatever their employer asks or else. Instead, you are responsible for making critical decisions to ensure the future success of all that is you. One of your key areas of accountability is determining how to protect one of your greatest assets—your ability to earn a living by leveraging your knowledge, skills, and expertise.

Your Words and Your Mindset

After you've chatted with your inner circle about your job situation, think about how you will talk about your layoff with the public at large. It's especially helpful to think about how you'll interact with those who don't know how layoffs work or give you unsolicited advice.

Here are a few suggested talking points to help you manage those potentially awkward interactions.

Talking About Your Current State and Near-Term Plans

You were not fired, discarded, cut loose, or shitcanned. These words tell the story that you did something terrible enough to get yourself fired or that you're mad because something awful was done to you. Instead, you were laid off, your job ended, your position was eliminated, or you were part of a company-wide reduction in force. It is just a thing that happened, and now you don't work at the place where you worked before.

You are not unemployed, an ex-employee of Big Important Tech Company, jobless, hopeless, or a big giant loser. Instead, you are in career transition, searching for your next opportunity, or looking for the job that is the right next step for you.

Talking About The Job You No Longer Have

Many times, people will make comments that might make you feel terrible about your current situation. While you can't control what other people say, you can control what you say in response and change that conversation. Here are a few ways you can shape your story.

The questions:

- I heard you're unemployed. What happened there?
- Your mom said you got fired.
- I heard you lost your job!

Helpful talking points:

- I got laid off. It happened a bit ago.
- I was part of a company-wide reduction in force at ABC Lending. My job ended on Tuesday.
- My job ended recently, along with about 100 others at the company.

Talking About What Is Next For You

The questions:

- What are you going to do now? I would be freaking out.

- I'd be scared to death if I were you. Are you sure you'll be okay?
- A person I sort of know lost their house/was unemployed for years/never worked again.

Helpful talking points:

- I'm making a plan for what to do next.
- I've had time to think about it and know my next steps.
- I am worried, but I know I'll be okay. I have a plan.

Talking About STILL Not Having a Job

The questions:

- So–do you have a job yet?
- Are you STILL unemployed?
- Did that thing you were interviewing for work out?

Helpful talking points:

- I'm talking to a few companies, and I'm sure something will work out soon.
- Finding a job can take a while. I'm making progress toward something new.
- Looking for a new role is now my main job.

Acknowledging People's Reassurances

The comments:

- Don't worry. It'll be fine.
- Hang in there! You're so talented!
- I'm praying for you.

Helpful talking points:

- Thanks.
- I appreciate that.
- I have adopted a Realistic Optimist mindset about this. It's helpful right now.

Addressing People's Well-Intentioned (and Sometimes Awful) Advice

The comments:

- You should just get a job as a bus driver/multi-marketing scheme salesperson/sign spinner.
- You should not settle for anything but the highest salary/the best title/ the corner office.
- You should go back to school/start your own consulting company/ have a baby/adopt many cats.
- You should just retire/give up because you are old/stop trying to get a job because ageism.
- You should downsize your house/sell your car/auction your jewelry/ maybe get a yurt.

Helpful talking points:

- I definitely have options. I'm determining my next steps.
- How about [the local sportsball team]! They are looking terrible/ adequate/great this year!
- Hey–look over there! [Followed by running away.]

Lesson Summary

Losing your job, even through no fault of your own, can be an ordeal. It impacts the very core of who you are as a person. As you work through this change, commit to processing your feelings so you can progress towards your goals. Experiencing those emotions will propel you forward.

Be kind to yourself as you work through the initial shock, anger, sadness, fear, and even relief. Dedicate yourself to acknowledging and working through feelings as they come. Remember, if you don't address your feelings, those emotions will probably come out during your job search as negativity, resentment, and blame.

In addition, remember to select your job search mindset. Adopting a Realistic Optimist mindset will help you balance the sometimes harsh realities of job searching with hope for the future. By staying mindful of what you can and can't directly control and shifting the words you use to describe your current state, you will have more success. These strategies will help you as you make well-informed business decisions in your new role as the CEO of You.

Your Next Steps

- Commit to acknowledging and experiencing your emotions throughout this process.
- Prioritize self-care activities to build your resilience.
- Choose a Realistic Optimist mindset and filter your experiences through that lens.

- Weigh your job search business decisions in your new role as the CEO of You.
- Align your words with your mindset.
- Decide which affirmations might work best for you and use them as needed.

Lesson Two: Keep your mind on your money (and your money on your mind).

No More Paychecks

After one layoff, I received the equivalent of several weeks of pay as severance. The good news was that my household had what we flippantly referred to as "a pile of money." There were several pieces of bad news, too. For one, that "pile of money" wasn't quite as big as we thought it would be after taxes were withheld. The other bad news was that there was no consistent paycheck coming into my household—a first for my family. Because of the aforementioned severance package, I wasn't eligible for unemployment payments yet. While having that "pile of money" instead of an empty bank account was definitely good, it was still unsettling looking at that amount and not knowing how long it would need to last.

Then there was health insurance. While my former employer earmarked some money to help cover interim healthcare costs, I still had to figure out what coverage I should get among the many options ranging from expensive but robust coverage to more reasonably priced but confusing options. Fortunately, "Obamacare" was now a thing—I just had to figure out where to start with all of that and use the state-run healthcare exchange website, which was also brand new and buggy.

The Importance of Keeping Your Mind on Your Money

I think it's safe to say that most people work to earn enough money to pay for their lives. Losing the salary and benefits associated with a job is decidedly life-altering. Even if you're not someone who usually has a written budget, you'll need to take a closer look at your financial life and shift your focus and priorities because of all the changes. This is also a case where ignoring these changes will end badly for you–possibly with overdraft fees, adverse impacts to your credit score, and maybe foreclosure or repossession. Even if this process feels scary, you'll have to do a few things to ensure your basic needs are covered, and you don't make moves that negatively impact your longer-term future.

A few tasks need attention within the first week after the layoff event. Addressing those core financial and healthcare decisions needs to be at the top of your priorities list. Fortunately, through my previous work experience and vast getting-laid-off school-of-hard-knocks education, I now feel comfortable navigating the pivot from an employed-person financial plan to a shorter-term survival budget.

My Assumptions

As I'm reviewing career transition finances and health insurance, I'm making a few assumptions about your financial life. I'm guessing you're reasonably responsible, but not perfect, with managing your money. You probably pay most of your bills on time, save a little for retirement, and have some debt. Regardless of the details of your finances while you were working, the purview of this chapter is to help you navigate from your layoff through when you have new paid work. My hope is that you're able to maintain basic continuity of life and not create a financial mess in the process.

Unemployment Length

Most people also wonder how long it will take them to find a new job after their layoff. The true and not helpful answer is that it depends. In my experience, my time between layoff day and starting a new job has ranged from just under two months to not quite nine months, with an average time of just over four months.

Let me skip ahead to the real question. How long should I plan to be in career transition? Personally, I would make a nine-month plan. Keep in mind, too, that unemployment insurance (UI) benefits typically last six months. I find it helpful to consider how your financial plan changes once that income stream ends. I'm also a "hope for the best, plan for the worst" contingency planner. Pick the length of time that makes the most sense for your household.

The Big Disclaimer

While I feel comfortable discussing various financial and insurance concepts, I do not currently hold a license or any certification that deems me inherently qualified to give financial advice. Therefore, the information provided here is intended for educational purposes only.

Sometimes, the core challenges are knowing how a system generally works, the terms used to describe what you're asking about, and where to go for additional help. Feel free to take my recommendations or not. Whatever you do, double-check my facts–and everyone's purported facts, for that matter. This is your life, and you will care more about your financial and healthcare decisions than anyone else. Use this information as a starting point for further research as you ultimately decide what's right for you.

Typical Gainfully Employed Person Budget Goals

When you're gainfully employed, you receive a couple of monthly paychecks. Your taxes are withheld based on the options you selected. You also may likely have deductions from each paycheck, which will include one or more of the following:

- Any employee portion of health insurance premiums for yourself and any covered family members.
- Any employee contributions to health savings plans, such as a Flexible Spending Account (FSA) or Health Savings Account (HSA).
- Any employee contributions to retirement plans, such as 401(k), 403(b).
- Any employee premiums for various and sundry benefits like supplemental life insurance, vision insurance, or a legal protection program.

During "normal" times, you probably have a few general financial goals. Chances are you think about where your money goes in a given month and look ahead to ways you'll spend, save, and share your money in the future. Your goals may look something like this:

- Pay for your needs, like food, shelter, utilities, and transportation.
- Spend money on those nice-to-haves that make life more enjoyable.
- Pay down debt.
- Save for short-term goals (like a vacation) and long-term goals (like retirement).
- Give to people and causes you care about.

Post-Layoff Changes

After a layoff, many things in your financial life change. Now, you don't know when your next paycheck will arrive or how much it might be. However, you do know that you need to figure out how to survive financially from now until that unknown future date. As you wrestle with uncertainty, you need to research options, run the numbers, and make the right decision for your household.

Managing Your Finances Helps You Feel More In Control

Maybe spending a lot of time thinking deep thoughts about your budget is not your happy place. Maybe it's scary at the best of times. However, now, this is going to be a necessity. Believe it or not, it will make you feel better knowing where you are and how things are going. I'm sure your imagination could catastrophize things that are way worse. It'll be a form of stress inoculation. Since you'll most likely be working with less income, it's crucial that you pay a little more attention to make sure you're not addressing your short-term financial state by creating bigger future problems.

Be a Realistic Optimist

Dealing with financial uncertainty can be stressful and draining. Between minimizing or eliminating some expenses in the short term and figuring out how to pay for healthcare needs, be sure to acknowledge that this next bit might be rough.

Remember, being realistic about the challenges you face and hopeful about the future will help you make more effective decisions. Doing an honest inventory of your current financial state may feel scary. However, even if your finances aren't where you want them to be, you will feel significantly better knowing where you are at. Then, you can use your energy to make a reality-based path forward.

Discuss Financial Changes With Your Household

When you go through a layoff, your whole household is impacted–including other financial decision-makers and children. Since you'll all be going through this together, it's important to talk about what is happening, what will change in the short term, and the why behind it all.

Make sure to discuss this with anyone else in your household who is making financial decisions. Discuss possible changes and agree on priorities and what will happen in the short term. Make sure you don't try to make changes for someone. Nothing makes for a less pleasant financial situation than multiple people working against a plan they never agreed with.

If you are in a situation where you share expenses with other people outside of your household, such as a child with a former spouse or partner, have a conversation to ensure you are aligned. Perhaps your child will not do as many extracurricular activities, or one of you will pick up more of the cost for a while. Insurance coverage may also be impacted, potentially causing one parent to add the child to their work-related healthcare plan. Be clear and collaborative as you decide how this will work.

In most cases, your household will have less money coming in. Consequently, you'll also likely take some steps to reduce spending. This may mean less takeout, continuing to use last year's baseball glove, and even canceling an already-planned trip. It might also mean more playing at playgrounds and fewer pricey amusement parks.

Being open and honest with your family members about what is changing is helpful. Personally, I've had "Momma's job ended" conversations with my child at ages 2, 10, 13, 15, 17, and 18. In the earliest conversation, I focused on our family being okay and we'd all be fine. Since we typically spent our time biking, playing board games, outdoor activities, movie nights, and reading, it didn't feel all that different—aside from fewer restaurant trips. Overall, I think letting children know what is happening is essential. Use this as a teachable moment where the whole family gets to practice adapting to life's changes as they come. More recently, when I shared my news about a layoff, I asked how everyone felt. The response from my daughter was an unphased, "This happens sometimes, and we're always fine."

Career Transition Financial Goals

Now, let's look at your new interim financial goals. Now, the focus is not on getting ahead or progressing toward larger goals. Instead, your overarching goal is to live through your period of unemployment until you are gainfully employed again with as little long-term financial trauma as possible. In this time of transition, your goals may look something like this:

- Pay monthly bills on time and in full (or make other arrangements).
- Prioritize basic short-term needs.
- Find inexpensive ways to enjoy life.
- Preserve your credit score.
- Tap savings as needed.
- Minimize the amount of debt you incur.

You are the CEO of You

As the CEO of You, it's time to think about how to manage this process's financial and health insurance aspects. This means making necessary business decisions to help you weather the storm. Like corporations sometimes do, you may need to do some temporary "layoffs" too. You might pause your gym membership, suspend the subscription on a video streaming service for a bit, or discontinue your wine of the month club purchases for a while.

Through all this, you get to decide your priorities and what makes the most sense for your household. Maybe Saturday movie theater night becomes Saturday movie-at-home night for a while. Perhaps visiting your favorite restaurant becomes a monthly rather than a weekly outing. As the CEO of You, determine what is your best course of action to ensure business continuity. Figure out what makes the most sense for you.

Career Transition Income Sources

While you won't have the income from your job on a go-forward basis, you may have one or more of these payments from your former employer after your position ends.

Your Last Paycheck

You will receive payment for any hours worked. Depending on your former employer, the timing and size of your last paycheck may vary. Typically, this final check will not include deductions for your health insurance premiums or other work-related benefits since you no longer participate in those programs. Taxes will also be withheld from that final paycheck. Be forewarned that your final paycheck may be smaller than you anticipated.

Remaining Paid Time Off (PTO), Sick Time, and Vacation Time

You may also be paid for PTO you have accrued but not yet taken. Depending on the company, your PTO may include separate allotments for sick time and vacation time. However, if your former employer had "unlimited" paid time off, you are unlikely to receive a vacation payout since there was no tie between accruing hours and taking that time off.

Some companies specify in their employee handbook that they do not pay out PTO after an employee no longer works there. However, many states require that employers pay out vacation to employees who reside in their state. Receiving a check to compensate you for unused PTO is not guaranteed, but it is worth inquiring with your former employer.

A Severance Package

In some cases, your former employer may offer you a severance package. Severance could include a lump sum, continuation of health insurance coverage for a set amount of time, and/or support services to help you find a new role outside of that organization. Realize companies do not have to provide a severance package when they do layoffs. If they offer you a severance package, it is often to minimize the likelihood of former employees taking legal action after a layoff. On a more altruistic note, it is also a way that companies help their former employees financially during a difficult transition time.

If you are offered a severance package, realize you will need to sign something before receiving a payment, benefits, or any other services promised. Once you sign, any thoughts you might have had about legal action regarding your employment with the organization are pretty much over. Read the agreement given to you, consider having a lawyer look it over, and ask for clarifications (and any revisions) before signing it. You also do not have to sign anything right away. I encourage you to sleep on it before you decide. In most cases, the company will give you a few days to a couple of weeks before you need to return the agreement. After that, there is typically a waiting period before you receive that money. In short, make sure that those details are in writing. This is big-time adulting here, so enlist help as needed.

If you do receive a severance payment, the amount can vary wildly. In fact, it could be between a fat lot of nothing, to the equivalent of a paycheck, to one to two weeks of pay for each year you were with the organization, to a larger check equaling months of income. It all depends on the organization, their financial position, how they want to be perceived during the layoff, or their general attitude toward former employees.

Also, know that there will be the amount they tell you the severance check will be (gross amount) and the amount you will actually receive (net amount). Since taxes are withheld, possibly even at a higher rate, depending on your situation, what you receive may be significantly less than expected.

Unemployment Insurance (UI) Benefits

In most cases, when your job ends due to a layoff, you will be eligible for unemployment insurance (UI) benefits. UI replaces a portion of your employed income. This money is intended to help you support yourself as you look for comparable new full-time work. Employers' payroll taxes fund the bulk of the money for each state's unemployment programs.

But Isn't Collecting Unemployment Just Lazy?

People regularly ask me if they should claim their unemployment benefits. Let me start with a story that illustrates the implications of not taking advantage of this short-term income stream.

A friend of mine had a sales operations job that ended due to a company-wide reduction in force. When she told her dad about her layoff and her plans to apply for unemployment, he commented, "We work for a living in this family," and that she shouldn't "be lazy" and live off government money she hadn't earned. Instead of applying for UI, she quickly found another job in a construction office. There, she worked 40 hours a week, made not quite half of what she earned before, and had no healthcare benefits. Soon, she struggled to pay her bills and fell behind on her rent and car payments. When she reached out to me for help, she was trying to ramp up her job search to find a better-paying job quickly so she wouldn't have to move back in with her parents.

I helped her with her resume and gave her a few job-searching ideas. Given her rigid work schedule, her next steps would be difficult. Since she had a new job, she was no longer eligible for unemployment. She also had a 40+ hour a-week commitment to a job with a rigid schedule where she would need to take unpaid time off to interview.

In short, I recommend you strongly consider taking your UI benefits and using them as intended–to help you bridge the gap between when your job ends and when you find a new job. Think of UI benefits as a paycheck for your most crucial interim job: working to find a new job aligned with your career goals and earning potential.

As the CEO of You, remember that this is a much-needed income stream to help you pay for your life in this time of transition.

UI Basics

Now, back to what UI is. Here are the basics regarding UI payments:

- Each state administers their own benefits. You can only collect benefits from one state at a time.
- The payment amount varies by state and will factor in your previous employment income.
- You complete a one-time online application to determine your eligibility and payment amount.
- There is often a waiting period before you receive your first payment.
- If you receive additional payments from your former employer (like severance or a vacation payout), these may affect the timing of your first payment.
- You may be able to set up tax withholding from your payments. UI income is typically taxable.
- Once they begin, payments are usually issued weekly, and you typically request each payment online or via phone.
- Doing paid work while receiving benefits may impact the amount of one or more payments.

- Benefits can last as long as 26 weeks (your maximum benefit period) and may vary by state.
- You are usually no longer eligible to receive payments when you are past your maximum benefit period or have a new job, whichever comes first.

Additional Requirements to Continue Receiving UI Payments

In many states, you'll be required to complete "reemployment activities" to ensure you are searching for a new role. Some states may require that you apply for a given number of jobs each week, sign up for that state's job search website, attend classes, and/or confirm each week that you did not turn down an offer of suitable work. If you're unsure how program parameters impact you, contact your state's unemployment office for clarification.

Other Income Options

There are multiple ways to pay for your life, varying from good to decidedly bad ideas. For example, you could use your emergency savings, your home equity line of credit, or take money out of your Health Savings Account (HSA). These may also have tax implications. You could also start a side hustle or take on paid short-term work. Depending on your age and the type of retirement savings plans, you may have the option to take some of the money out without penalty. You could also sell items you don't use, create a fundraising page, rely on credit cards, incur additional debt, or take a withdrawal from your retirement plan and pay a steep penalty. Whatever options you choose, consider the short- and long-term implications of those decisions before taking your next steps.

Career Transition Healthcare

While you're working, your health insurance has a pretty good chance of being connected to your day job. You make coverage choices when you start that job and, after that, once a year during open enrollment. You may have a few choices to make—like who will be covered and possibly choosing one of a handful of options on your coverage—but your company has already selected the main choices for you. Your employer pays for part of it, facilitates the payment to the insurance company, and often even gives you the ability to set up and use a Health Savings Account (HSA) or a Flexible Spending Account (FSA) as a separate benefit—even though it seems like it's a part of your health insurance. Get ready to appreciate all the work employers do to help their employees obtain and pay for health insurance.

Health Insurance Options

After you are laid off, your former employer will let you know when your employer-paid health insurance benefits end. It may be as soon as your last day of work (also known as your separation date), the end of the calendar month, or some other date altogether. If you have the time and ability to do so, fit in any doctor's appointments, dental cleanings, or prescription refills you have been putting off while you still have coverage in effect.

Once your employer-sponsored health insurance ends, you have some choices to make. Researching, evaluating, and choosing how to handle your healthcare costs and what makes sense for you and yours is its own special ordeal. Remember that you can also choose to go without health insurance and assume the risk of paying for any possible expenses. While there is no longer a federal penalty for not having healthcare coverage in the United States, individual states may have their own rules. Even so, carefully consider available options and choose the one that makes the most sense for you and your household. Here are a few common options.

Continued Health Insurance as Part of a Severance Package

As I mentioned, as a part of your severance package, you may receive continued health insurance for a specified time period. This could be the company continuing to pay for the benefits you had before or giving you money intended to help you pay for health insurance. These are two very different propositions.

If the company continues to pay for your health insurance, your coverage will work like before with the exact costs, pharmacies, and doctors you visited. This may include the company logistically paying your bill or with you receiving monthly invoices and making the payments. However, if you receive money to pay for healthcare coverage, you will need to decide what to purchase, enroll, and then pay for it as billed.

COBRA and Continuation Coverage

COBRA (Consolidated Omnibus Budget Reconciliation Act) is a provision that allows former employees to keep their previously work-sponsored health insurance and cover the total cost. If you choose this option, you can usually keep the same healthcare coverage for up to 18 or 36 months. As part of your layoff paperwork, you will receive information about the logistics, associated costs, and the deadline for signing up.

The good news? Your coverage doesn't change. The bad news? The cost may knock you back. Now, you'll pay the full amount for your coverage instead of your employer helping offset the total amount. For example, while working, you may have spent $500 per month on your household's health insurance. With COBRA, you could pay thousands of dollars per month for that same coverage. In some cases, like if it's late in the year and you are close to having paid your deductible, it may make sense to consider COBRA.

Become a Dependent on Someone Else's Employer Plan

Depending on your age and personal situation, you may have the option to be added to someone else's employer-sponsored health insurance plan. Here are two common scenarios:

- If you are under 26 years old, you may be eligible to be added to a parent's health insurance.
- If you have a spouse or domestic partner, you may be eligible to be added to their health insurance. Some plans might strictly add legal spouses, while others may have less stringent requirements.

If your former employer's healthcare plan covered you, your family member's employer healthcare plan usually allows you to enroll, even mid-year. Be sure to check with your family member's employer to see if being added to their plan is available and if it's the right option for you.

Remember, if you are added to your family member's health insurance plan, the additional costs for whoever is footing the bill can elicit a response varying from "'No big deal." to "Holy crap! That's a whole lotta extra money each paycheck!"

This is the option I have chosen whenever it has been available to me. Your situation may differ, so make the choice that makes the most sense for you.

Healthcare.gov: The Marketplace

Since the introduction of the federal Affordable Care Act (ACA), additional health insurance options with at least a minimum level of coverage have been available outside of employer-sponsored health insurance plans. To find out what health insurance options are available, your eligibility, and any amount of help (in the form of a subsidy) you might qualify for, check out Healthcare.gov (also referred to as "The Marketplace"). Alternatively, some states have their own healthcare-specific website, like MNsure.gov in Minnesota. Regardless of the website your state uses, this is the go-to place to find out about possible healthcare options that comply with ACA standards, meaning that they include a base level of coverage (like preventative health screenings, emergency services, pregnancy, etc.).

Many of these plans are High Deductible Health Plans (HDHP). The higher the deductible, the lower your monthly premium, but the higher the possible out-of-pocket expense you will have. As with other high deductible plans, you can save money in a separate Health Savings Account (HSA) to help cover those expenses. However, Healthcare.gov does not have the option to help you set up an HSA account, so you'll need to seek out a financial institution to help you set up that type of account if you are interested.

One significant benefit of looking on Healthcare.gov is the possibility of getting a subsidy. A subsidy will help offset your healthcare cost and is usually applied before any premium you would need to pay every month. Typically, subsidies are calculated based on your year's projected income, and details may vary from state to state. You would need to enroll in an ACA plan within 60 days of being laid off. Some people may opt for a Healthcare.gov plan because of a pre-existing condition. Remember to do your research and make the choice that is right for your unique situation.

Overall, Healthcare.gov can be a lot to navigate. Fortunately, they do have help available in the form of agents, brokers, or assisters. These people can answer your questions and help you choose the healthcare coverage that makes the most sense for your household.

Short-Term Health Insurance

Short-term health insurance is just that—insurance intended to help you bridge a few months' gap between other longer-term healthcare coverage. Typically, these plans don't include preventative benefits (like annual physicals or flu shots), but the cost is significantly lower. This kind of coverage ensures that if something catastrophic happens, like an accident where you end up in the hospital, you won't go broke in the process.

During one period of unemployment, I bought short-term health insurance coverage for my daughter (for a tumultuous month where, for a moment, it looked like my daughter would be in a position where neither her dad nor I would have access to health insurance through an employer). It was under $100 per month and ensured she had at least some coverage as we figured out her longer-term health insurance. Enrolling and canceling these plans is also relatively quick and straightforward.

To purchase a plan like this, do an online search for short-term health insurance in your state. Double-check what each plan covers and how it is rated compared to other available plans.

Other Healthcare Options

Just like with income streams, there are multiple ways to pay for your healthcare needs, varying from good to decidedly bad ideas. For example, you could buy a private health insurance plan, enroll in Medicare if you are eligible, participate in Medicaid/medical assistance based on your financial situation, visit community health centers, or use telehealth. In addition, you could pay for any expenses you incur using money previously saved in a health savings account, a healthcare-specific credit card, and discount cards to minimize prescription costs.

When it comes down to it, consider the short and long-term implications of your healthcare decisions before choosing your course of action. One of these is the possible financial hardship of having a life-altering medical diagnosis or expense without being insured. Remember to assess the options and make the right choice for your household.

Career Transition Expenses

Unfortunately, while your regularly scheduled income goes away, your expenses generally do not. Now, it's more a matter of adjusting your priorities and seeing what you can do to streamline your layoff survival budget. Remember, your overarching goal is to live through your period of unemployment until you are gainfully employed again with as little financial trauma as possible.

Prioritizing Expenses

When times are tight, you will need to make more calculated decisions regarding where you spend money. Here is a recommendation for prioritizing which bills you pay when money is tight:

- Rent or mortgage payments.
- Transportation.

- Phone.
- Internet access.
- Utilities: electricity, gas, heat.
- Food.
- Minimum debt payments.

Paring Down Expenses

This is also an excellent time to see what expenses you can pare down in the short term to ensure that the money you do have lasts a little longer. Here are a few ideas:

- Comparison shop for car insurance, Internet access, and other essential bills where costs might be negotiable.
- Review paid subscriptions and memberships and pause or cancel those you can temporarily live without.
- Get a public library card. Services available can significantly reduce your spending on books, streaming services, movies, online learning, magazines, and audiobooks.
- Plan your meals and buy groceries more mindfully to minimize waste.
- Meet people more often for coffee or a drink than dinner. Even better, meet people for a walk.
- Do more outdoor activities and free online exercise videos and fewer paid in-person classes.
- Take fewer flying vacations and more driving day trips to local destinations or overnight trips to stay with friends and family.

Plan Your Fun

When money is tight, you may want to go extreme and cut out everything non-essential. While it may seem logical from a dollars and cents perspective, denying yourself is not a great long-term strategy. Make sure you take care of yourself during this process—part of which is making sure you still do things you enjoy and have fun. Personally, I'm a fan of $5 Tuesday movie night, $4 night at the roller rink, and getting outside more often. Make sure you build enjoyable activities into your routine instead of focusing only on the stressful parts of your temporary financial situation.

Remember, too, that this is a time when you may have more time than money. That might mean that while you're in career transition, you spend the time grocery shopping and cooking at home instead of paying for the convenience of delivery services and restaurants. As the CEO of You, decide what makes the most sense for your household.

Expenses You May Need to Keep

Remembering that unemployment is typically a short-term problem lasting under a year is essential. While minimizing expenses is valuable, don't make big, short-sighted decisions to solve temporary problems. Here are three examples of what not to do:

- **Childcare:** If your children are in daycare, it may seem like a good idea to pull them out while you are in between jobs. Realize that your new job is looking for a job, which means you need time to focus on applying for new roles, making new professional connections, and interviewing with potential employers. These activities are more challenging when you're trying to parent at the same time. Furthermore, finding daycare for your children again when you are ready to start working full-time may be nearly impossible.
- **Current housing:** When you look at where your money goes each month, paying for the roof over your head is likely your biggest expense. You—or a well-meaning family member—may suggest moving to a smaller apartment or selling your house to save money. While you certainly could do that, remember that finding a new place to live and orchestrating a move takes time, energy, and money. Decide if the effort required to make that change is worth the money you might save. Also, decide if you'll be happy with that change once you are employed again.
- **Transportation:** Your personal vehicle is probably one of your biggest expenses. You may wonder if you should trade your car for a less expensive model or go without a car. As you evaluate options, think about where you will need to go and the implications of operating

without on-demand transportation of your own. Consider the cost and availability of alternatives like public transportation, ride-sharing, car rentals, or people willing to help get you from place to place. Depending on where you live, where you need to go, and how much extra time you can commit to making these trips, these may or may not be feasible options. In addition, selling and/or buying a car will also take time, energy, and money.

These possible courses of action all have one thing in common. They may seem wise in the short term when you're trying to minimize your expenses. However, they may also be decisions you'll regret, which may take longer to undo in the future. Consider these larger decisions in the context of your longer-term plans. Don't choose a more permanent solution for a temporary problem. You may do more harm than good to your longer-term financial life. In addition, the time and effort you spend on any of these activities could be better used to take steps toward finding a new job.

When Income and Expenses Don't Line Up

One of the harsh realities of career transition is that your current income may be significantly lower than your outgo. In these cases, you need to consider your options. In addition to paring down expenses where you can, it may include finding an interim job to help pay core bills. It could also involve taking on additional debt. If taking on debt seems the likely option, when you are reemployed, one of your priorities will be to start paying down that debt.

What To Do if You Can't Pay Your Core Bills

If you can't pay your bills, call the company and discuss possible alternatives to paying your entire bill. Instead of just plain NOT paying a bill, make a phone call. I know this can be hard and humbling, but it is vital to figure out a plan. Remember, you're not the first person to be in a position where they had an unexpected job loss and needed to figure out alternatives. It is also to the company's advantage to work with you. It's in the company's interest to help you stay on track as a customer rather than for them to spend the time and staffing on repossessing items or turning off and on utilities. Help them help you.

Making this call also helps minimize damage to your credit score (which could even impact your ability to find work in some cases). One of the most significant contributing factors to your credit score is paying your bills on time. Be sure to call right away when you start to have problems making payments rather than when utilities are about to be shut off. I encourage you to talk with your mortgage company when you worry about having difficulty making one mortgage payment instead of waiting until you face foreclosure. Remember—even if you have waited, MAKE THAT CALL!

When working with a company on making some sort of payment arrangement, you may be able to defer payments, figure out a payment plan, take advantage of a company-sponsored program, or find a government-sponsored program to help you during a hard time. County, faith-based organizations, and non-profits may be able to help you, too. Whether you need help paying for gas, food, transportation, or utilities, use the available resources. Taking this action frees up your thoughts from worry to problem-solving.

Lesson Summary

Layoffs bring fundamental changes to your financial life. Not only does your predictable stream of income end, but your benefits, including your health insurance, also take a hit. Discuss these changes with your household so everyone is on board as you make short-term adjustments. Review the many health insurance options available and decide which makes the most sense for your household in the near term. Be sure to leverage interim income streams, including unemployment insurance, to help you maintain so you can find new paid work that supports your life going forward.

Your Next Steps

- Talk with members of your household about financial and insurance changes
- Think about your career transition financial goals.
- Review and decide your next steps on any severance agreement you may receive.
- Apply for Unemployment Insurance (UI) benefits in your state.
- Think about other possible career transition income streams.
- Research and select the right options for paying for healthcare costs for your household.
- Minimize your expenses where possible.
- Figure out how to still have fun.
- As needed, make a phone call to make payment arrangements.

Lesson Three: Ask yourself, "What do you want to be next?"

I Want Something Else

When I was laid off from three jobs in a row, I didn't do much (if any) heavy thinking about what I wanted next. In short, one position ended, and I found a similar role with the same kind of company until I was laid off once again. After three go-rounds, I realized I owed it to myself to step back and reassess. I needed to make better choices—or at least different mistakes. I hated the term burnout—but I was pretty sure I was completely and utterly burned out. I was also certain it was not where I wanted to end up again.

Post-layoff, I recovered for a few days. Then I started to think about what was next for me. Since my layoff was so fresh in my brain, I started with what I didn't want:

- I did not want to work in such a volatile industry.
- I did not want a high-pressure role where I was constantly beating my head against a wall as I tried to "do more with less."
- I didn't want to be the boss right now.

Then, I started thinking about what I wanted:

- I wanted a larger organization with a bigger training team.
- I wanted a well-diversified company with multiple income streams so it would be less subject to market volatility.
- I wanted to work as an individual contributor on a team.
- I wanted a competitive salary, a job that leveraged my skills, and to work remotely.
- I wanted to use my expertise in supporting software and my knowledge of the financial, healthcare, or insurance industries.
- I wanted to design training, run projects, collaborate with subject matter experts, and deliver instructor-led training.

Within a few weeks, I accepted a job offer that met those requirements.

An Opportunity for Self-Reflection

While having your job end because of someone else's choice is always frustrating, finding the opportunity in a less-than-ideal situation is essential. While it's hard to take the time to reflect when you're busy living your life, a layoff means the pause button has just been pushed on your career. This may be your once-in-a-lifetime chance to reassess your current situation and think about what you really want from your work life.

Challenge yourself to think about the following questions:
- What do I want to be next? How might I leverage what I do in a place that would be a better fit?
- What are all the jobs? What exists now that may not have been an option the last time I looked?
- Which type of job might be right for me? What's out there that is the same or different from my previous jobs?

As you prepare to launch your post-layoff job search, think beyond your next role and about your bigger, longer-term work goals. You may have a job title in mind, a specialty, a preferred industry, or want to focus on solving a specific type of problem. You may want more flexibility, structure, accountability, or freedom in how you do what you do. You may also want to do something completely different from what you've done or use your skills in a new way.

My goal for this chapter is to encourage you to really think about what you want to do instead of automatically getting a new job just like your last job. You'll either affirm that you are doing the kind of work that resonates with you or give you valuable insights into what you should shift to improve your overall job satisfaction.

What Do You Want To Be When You Grow Up?

When I talk with small children, I often ask them what they want to be when they grow up because their answers are always kind of amazing. Their dream jobs vary from firefighter to rock star to a dinosaur. The best answer I ever heard was from my daughter when she was three years old. She responded, "I don't know, Momma. What are all of the jobs?" Well played, young lady. Well played.

As adults, we must each look at our work and ask ourselves again, "What do I want to be when I grow up?"

Now is the time for you to do some soul-searching on what you really want to do in your next job. If you loved your last job, think about what specifically you loved. If you hated your last role, reflect on what you hated and want instead. By thinking about what you want your next job to look like, from the type of company to your day-to-day duties to the pay and benefits, you are taking one step closer to making your ideas a reality.

When I look at people who struggle to find a new role, they are often unable to explain clearly and concisely what they want. Sometimes, I think people are trying to be open to multiple things in hopes it will make them more employable. Perhaps counterintuitively, people tend to land faster if they figure out what they want and then showcase their skills as a solid fit for that position. In short, figure out what you want so you can pursue the kind of work that aligns with who you are, what you want from work, and the type of life you'd like to have.

Your Early Career "What I Want To Be When I Grow Up" Decision

I suspect that many people decide early on what type of job they want and continue on that path as long as it is going mostly okay. It's easy to stay put when you're making a reasonable salary, working with okay-ish people, and doing a job you like well enough.

Among groups of adults, a common topic of conversation is complaining about work. Whether it's the annoying coworker, the out-of-date computers, or how no one listens to their ideas, the undertow of general discontent is ever-present. It's also less "Maybe I should find something else" and more "This is just how it is." It's also hard to proactively change when you have a good enough job. It's much easier to contend with "the devil you know" since it's always easier to keep doing what you are doing instead of taking risks and exploring other options.

What Do You Want to Be Next?

Once you have thought about your longer-term goals, you should also ask yourself, "What do I want to be next?" Make sure whatever you decide to pursue next is aligned with what you want to be when you grow up.

Some people are fortunate to have found the right focus area for them. Others may have liked parts of their job but wished they had a different type of manager, worked for a more ethical company, or had a little more responsibility. Now is your chance to evaluate your previous work experiences and use that information to learn about what you'd like to pursue in the future.

Let's look at a few strategies for helping you determine what you want to be next.

You are the CEO of You

As the CEO of You, think about your long-term goals. Just like the CEO of the company does not make decisions based on what other companies think they should do, you need to do the same. Regardless of other people's opinions, make the right decision for you and your household. Align your next steps with your overall goals. Think in terms of preferences and priorities.

Remember, too, that you're not just the CEO of your career but the CEO of all aspects of you. This means not taking "any old job" unless you decide that is the right move for you overall. This also means that your business decisions may change over time as the environment changes. You can also change your mind on the right job for you based on the length of your job search and other factors in your life.

Structured Soul Searching

Here are a few activities to help you discover who you are, what matters to you, your talents, strengths, and interests. Taking an inventory of those skills will help you answer those questions about what you want to be next.

For additional information on this structured soul searching process, including links to the resources mentioned, visit **TheLayoffLady.com/ SoulSearching**.

Your Values

When you contemplate the future, it's good to revisit what really matters to you at your very core. Thinking about your values is a great place to start.

Identifying what matters to you is helpful whether you're thinking about how you spend your money, what kinds of activities appeal to you, whom you want to spend time with, and (go figure) what type of work you want to do. It can also be challenging to start from nothing and think of the right words to articulate those high-level ideals that matter to you.

Values Identification Exercise

I discovered the think2perform Online Values Exercise in a previous job where I was teaching people about whole-person health and financial wellness. It's a great tool to help stimulate your thinking about what really matters to you.

The assessment includes 51 named value cards and four rounds of reviewing the cards. The total time to complete this activity is about 15 minutes. Depending on how much contemplation you do during the process, you may want to allow extra time. In the end, you'll have five value cards with descriptions that name and describe critical areas that matter to you.

To access this free online values exercise, use your favorite search engine to find "think2perform Online Values Exercise." You can also visit **TheLayoffLady.com/SoulSearching** for additional details.

After completing the exercise, note your top five values. Think about your previous roles, and answer the following questions to learn more about each of your identified values:

- What led me to prioritize this value?
- What does this value mean to me?
- How do I strive to live this value?
- How do I want to use this value more?

Reflect on how each value influences what you choose to do. Specifically, think about how it plays out in your work.

How My Values Look In Practice

One of my top five values is autonomy. At work, I like to be able to decide what projects to work on, schedule my time, and choose how to complete tasks. I want to have the option to work longer on a project when I hit flow or when a deadline is on the horizon. I also like to be able to come in later or leave earlier on other days as long as I'm getting my work done. I must be trusted, accountable for my results, and free from micromanagement.

Finding work that aligns with what you care about helps improve your overall happiness.

Your Strengths

Now that you've considered what you value, you'll shift your focus to your talents. If you are like many people, you probably aren't always consciously aware of what you are truly good at. It's likely that you just do what you do, and you may not realize that not everyone thinks, acts, or solves problems quite the way you do.

Let's look at a few ways to identify what you are good at and the unique value proposition you bring to a potential employer.

Assessing Your Strengths

It's hard to beat Gallup's strengths-related tools and resources when identifying your natural talents and how they show up. For a very reasonable price, the CliftonStrengths® Assessment (previously known as the Clifton StrengthsFinder or StrengthsFinder 2.0) helps you identify your top strengths. It gives you language to talk about your unique skills. Since this is a tool many companies use, using strengths terminology can help you and potential employers understand one another.

This 30-minute online assessment costs about $20 and includes 177 questions. Each question consists of two statements, and you use a scale to select which of the two statements is more like you. From there, you'll receive a report listing your top five strengths and a personalized description of what those strengths look like for you. Reading this report about yourself (a freakishly accurate one) can be downright life-changing.

After taking the assessment, you'll be able to see your talents and have the language to explain how what you do sets you apart from others. Having a way to put your abilities into words can translate directly into your resume, and how you talk about who you are and what you bring to the table is invaluable as you decide what you want to be next and as you talk about what you can do.

Your personalized report will include a list of your top 5 strengths, a general description of each strength, and statements specific to how this strength looks for you. Since Gallup's strengths model is popular in corporate

America, you'll also have the language to talk about what you are good at, which should resonate with many employers.

To access this online strengths assessment, use your favorite search engine to find the "CliftonStrengths® Assessment."

Strengths and How My Strengths Show Up

One of my CliftonStrengths® top five strengths is Learner.

Here is the general description of what that strength means:

"You have a great desire to learn and want to improve continuously. The process of learning, rather than the outcome, excites you."

Here is one of the personalized Strengths Insights from my CliftonStrengths® results, which is ridiculously accurate for me:

"By nature, you acquire knowledge more easily when discussing ideas, concepts, or theories. Thoughts come alive for you when questions are posed, and answers are proposed. You have a delightful time thinking aloud and listening to intelligent people express themselves. You naturally document or store in your mind bits and pieces of discussions. You want to refer to these insights or facts whenever the opportunity presents itself."

Here's what this strength looks like in my regularly scheduled life:

I am always taking notes in day-to-day conversations. Usually, I'll leave even the most casual conversation with a new restaurant to try out, a band to listen to, a word to look up, or a broad idea to learn more about. I'm always learning whatever happens to present itself, and I love talking with smart people about their areas of interest or expertise.

Here is what this strength looks like in my career:

As a Learner, I have taken roles in multiple industries, knowing that I'd learn the business along the way. Through different jobs, I now know how travel agents upsell excursions to cruise customers, the importance of the windshield to the structural integrity of a vehicle, the strategic value of the clergy housing allowance exclusion for pastors, and best practices for mortgage underwriting.

A greater understanding of your unique strengths and how they manifest will help you discuss the value you could bring to an organization.

Collect Colleague Feedback

Along with taking assessments, talking to people about their experiences interacting with you is an invaluable way to learn more about your skills and strengths.

Schedule time to talk with a colleague. Ask for their feedback on what they think you do well, where they have seen you excel, and times when they have seen you struggle at work. Be sure to ask them what they learned working with you and what they think your superpower is. Through this interaction, you'll learn lessons about your skill set from someone who has had several opportunities to observe you in action.

I have a former coworker I have had the pleasure of working with at three organizations. I have interacted with him as a student in a new hire class, as a coworker in the same department, and as my direct report and trusted advisor. He not only has several first-hand experiences working with me, but he also has insights and gives me the kind of clear and direct feedback I need. He commented on specific techniques I used to design courses, his observation that I liked instructional design more than managing people, and pointed out times when he'd noticed my frustrations. Our conversations about our shared experiences added new dimensions to how I understand and describe my approach to my work.

Gather Insights From Previous Positions

In addition to your strengths, it's valuable to know your work-related preferences. One great way to identify your work likes and dislikes is to reflect on your previous positions and what you liked and disliked about your past jobs. Ask yourself the following questions about jobs you've had in the past, and note your answers:

What You Thought Went Well

- What made you look forward to going to work at this employer?
- What was most satisfying about this job?
- What were you good at in this job?
- How did your manager help you grow? Find joy in your work? Build trust?

What You Would Change

- What did you find frustrating about this employer?
- What parts of this job were disappointing?
- Which parts of this job were most difficult? Were they challenges that you enjoyed? Did they get easier over time?
- What did your manager do (or not do) that reduced your effectiveness?

Use the answers to these questions to help you discover what you want and don't want in your next role.

Insights Example: My Insights

Here is an example insights reflection from one of my previous jobs:

What I Thought Went Well

- What made you look forward to going to work at this employer?

I liked that it was a larger employer that I perceived as being more stable. I liked that my paychecks didn't bounce. I enjoyed working with the person who sat next to me.

- What was most satisfying about this job?

I liked that I was tasked with creating and rolling out a mentoring program and career paths for multiple IT department roles.

- What were you good at in this job?

I was good at building relationships with stakeholders and garnering buy-in for programs I was implementing.

- How did your manager help you grow? Find joy in your work? Build trust?

My boss wanted to be helpful. She scheduled weekly team meetings so we all knew about company initiatives and priorities.

What I Would Change

- What did you find frustrating about this employer?

I disliked the rigidity. They used antiquated software that was hard to use. It was also a company culture that used practical jokes to show inclusion, and I did not like that.

- What parts of this job were disappointing?

I disliked my lack of autonomy on the projects I was supposed to lead.

- Which parts of this job were most difficult? Were they challenges that you enjoyed? Did they get easier over time?

I was not good at managing my relationship with my boss and selling her on my project vision. I'm not sure if this would have gotten better with time.

- What did your manager do (or not do) that reduced your effectiveness?

My boss was a micromanager who scheduled appointments with me each week to help me plan my calendar.

Overarching Insights

This exercise reminded me to think more critically about my organizational fit before accepting a new role. I also realized the value I place on influencing organizational decision-making and working consultatively.

Completing this reflection for your previous jobs will increase your understanding of your likes, dislikes, and work style preferences. You can use these insights while networking with people, which will empower them to keep an eye out for a role and organization that might be a good fit for you. In addition, you can use these insights to help you select roles that seem like a good choice for you and ask better questions during the interview process.

What Do You Want for Compensation?

Now that you understand your target job and what that looks like, think about the level and kind of compensation in a job. This will include the money you will earn and the benefits provided, perks, and opportunities you value. First, let's talk about the actual compensation package.

Factors That In luence Your Target Salary Range

When considering your salary requirements, I suggest using a range instead of one specific number. Let's look at strategies for determining your target salary range.

Here are numbers you might have in mind that could impact your range:

- What you need to make to pay your core monthly bills.
- The absolute minimum salary you are willing to accept.
- What you need based on your budget, savings plan, and financial goals.
- The minimum salary you would happily accept.
- What you've made previously.
- What colleagues make.

- What you've seen listed in current job postings.
- What you think you are worth.
- What you would like to make.
- What you'd be really excited about making.
- Your dream salary.

I suggest the salary range you share with potential employers starts with the low-end number, which is the **minimum salary you would happily accept**, and the high-end number is **what you'd be really excited about**. If you are applying for more than one type of role, you may have a salary range for each type of work.

What the Marketplace is Paying

Knowing what the market will bear should also factor into your target salary range. Here are a few strategies for finding out more:

Search for Open Positions in States With Pay Transparency Laws

Job openings may give you additional insights into benefits offered and pay rates. As more and more companies include salary information for open roles, it becomes easier to understand the value a given company might place on a role.

To understand what an employer might pay for a specific role, search for your target job title on your favorite job search website. Look for open positions that include salary information. Consider searching for your target job titles in larger cities in states with pay transparency laws.

I usually search for roles in Denver, Colorado, or San Francisco, California, as a starting point. Once you find a position that closely matches your target job title, note the minimum and maximum salary range numbers and any descriptors the company has on what qualifications would push a candidate toward the upper end of the salary range. From there, as needed, use a cost of living calculator to adjust the minimum and maximum numbers for each role in your local job market. Use your favorite search engine to find "Pay Transparency Laws" and the current year for the most up-to-date information on this topic.

Research Your Job Title and Geographic Location

Salary.com and Payscale.com are two websites that focus on salary information that recruiters highly recommend. In fact, Salary.com has a Know Your Worth calculator where you can add details like your job title, location, education level, and years of experience and see the impact each factor has on your potential market value.

Additional Factors

Here are a few factors that might make this process challenging:

- Salaries vary by geographic region, job title, and individual company.
- Not all companies include salary information on job postings.
- Some companies adjust salaries by geographical area for the same role, while others do not.
- Titles are not used consistently across organizations. Titles may have varying responsibilities as well as salary levels.
- Company benefits can range from few and expensive to plentiful and low cost. Benefit costs can impact your take-home pay significantly.
- Some companies will pay lower or higher than the salary information you find.
- Just because your skill set has a specific value according to a website, that does not mean that a given employer needs your level of skill for their open position or that they are willing to pay for your level of expertise. Consequently, the salary for any given role may be lower than your target salary range.

Total Compensation Components

If you are working in a contract role, one with no other benefits, your hourly rate and your salary are the same. When you are working a full-time position for a company, in addition to the money you receive in the form of your paycheck, your actual salary, there are usually additional components to your total compensation. Let's break it down a little further.

The Actual Money

First, let's look at a high-level, generalized overview of the money you may receive as a part of a total compensation package for a full-time benefits-eligible role:

- **Base salary:** Money you will earn for showing up and meeting basic employer expectations for your job. This is typically paid on a bi-weekly or bi-monthly basis. This is usually what recruiters are asking for when they inquire about your "salary requirements."
- **Bonus:** Additional money you may (or may not) receive based on the performance of you individually, your team, and/or the organization as a whole. Bonus payment depends on the organization and may be paid quarterly, annually, or on another schedule.
- **Commission:** Additional money you may earn, typically based on what and how much you sell. Commissions are often a percentage of what you have sold. Bonus payment depends on the organization and may be paid monthly, quarterly, or on another schedule.
- **Signing bonus:** Additional money you may receive for agreeing to work for a given company outside of your agreed-upon salary. This is usually a one-time payment paid out as an incentive to accept a job offer.

Paid Time Off

Employers also often pay you for specific hours when you do not work. Here are a few standard categorizations for different types of paid time off: paid time off (PTO), sick time, vacation time, paid holidays, floating holidays, volunteer time, bereavement leave, jury duty pay, or military leave.

Instead of having a specific number of paid days available for sick or vacation time, some companies have unlimited time off policies. In most cases, instead of earning and then choosing to use paid time off, you work with your manager whenever you want to use this benefit. Generally, as long as you perform your job to an acceptable level, you can take time off.

Employer Money for a Specific Purpose

In addition to receiving money in the form of a check or payment payable to you, you may also receive money earmarked for a specific purpose. This could include a contribution to your retirement account, health savings account, or reimbursement for professional development. Companies might also give you a stipend to offset your costs for various expenses including a gym membership, home office setup, internet access, a cell phone plan, uniforms, your passport, mileage, lunch, parking, travel, rent, or student loan payments. Often, people overlook the out-of-pocket savings or additional long-term value of these benefits.

Insurance and Benefits, at Least Partially Employer Paid

In the United States, many people obtain different types of insurance through their employers. Employers often pay administration costs of the plan and help cover part of the premium.

Health Insurance is usually the big ticket item when it comes to employee benefits. Employers may offer one or more health insurance plan options and usually cover administrative costs and part of the monthly premiums. Costs will vary widely. When reviewing benefit premium costs offered by different potential employers, I saw that health insurance rates for my family of three range from $255.00 per month to $1,249.30 per month. Keep this in mind when sharing your target salary range with a potential employer.

Additional insurance benefits may be offered as fully or partially employer-paid. These include dental insurance, life insurance, short-term disability insurance, and long-term disability insurance. In addition, employers may pay for access to an Employee Assistance Program (EAP) and flexible spending accounts for employees to save money to help cover healthcare, dependent care, and transportation costs.

Access to Purchase Additional Benefits

Many employers offer the option for employees to purchase additional benefits. These can include vision insurance, short-term disability, long-term disability, enhanced disability coverage, supplemental life insurance, spouse life insurance, child life insurance, accident insurance, condition-specific health insurance, a legal protection plan, or orthodontic benefits.

Perks

Companies may also offer a variety of perks. Perks can be anything that makes work easier, more engaging, or more pleasant. Many offices may include free beverages, snacks, and meals. Additional perks could include shift bidding, flexible work arrangements, remote work, work-from-home days, summer hours, four-day workweeks, onsite flu shots, overtime opportunities, or company events.

These can also include items you can purchase for a lower cost or resources you can take advantage of that you might otherwise pay for elsewhere. These could include an onsite gym, onsite daycare, free parking, entertainment discounts, stamps, bus passes, use of the company van, cell phone plan discounts, or reduced entry fees for area attractions.

The Salary Question: Revisited

Remember, when a recruiter asks about your salary, there is a lot more going on than just your base salary. In most cases, recruiters are asking you only about your base salary as defined above. Realize that two jobs with the same base salary can have wildly different total compensation packages.

Overall, I suggest giving a salary range instead of a set number to account for possible differences in company-offered benefits. I also suggest letting the recruiter know that you may adjust your salary range accordingly as you learn more about the role.

Prioritize What Matters to You

When determining what the next right role is for you, it's always a balancing act between many factors. Job responsibilities, commute, and salary are usually top considerations. Beyond those basics, people may prioritize some aspects more than others. For example, some may place a high value on having a specific job title, receiving tuition reimbursement money to earn their next credential, and opportunities for promotions. Someone else may prioritize having exciting work, schedule flexibility, the ability to work remotely most days, and low health insurance premiums. Still another person may be most interested in working alongside colleagues in an office, having the opportunity to mentor new hires, and finding a job they can keep for the next decade or more. As you evaluate possible employment options, keep in mind what means the most to you.

Make Your Preferences List

Now that you've reflected in a few different ways, it's time to gather what you've learned and use that to put together your preferences list for the job you want. Note your answers to these questions:

Work Logistics

- Are you interested in a full-time, part-time, contract, or freelance job? How many hours do you want to work a week? What work hours and schedule would you prefer?
- Would you like to work in-person, part in-person and part remotely (hybrid), or all remote?
- How many miles/minutes would you be comfortable commuting? How often would you want to commute?
- Would you like to travel for work? If so, how frequently?

Salary and Benefits

- What base salary would you like?
- Would you expect a bonus or commission? What might that look like?
- How much time off would you like?
- What benefits matter most to you? What would be nice to have?

The Employer

- What field or fields would you like to work in?
- What size of a company or industry would you like to work for?
- What company culture aligns with what you want your work life to be like?
- What do you want in your immediate manager?

The Job Itself

- What job titles might be a good fit for you?
- Would you like a manager role, individual contributor role, or player/coach role (doing both)?
- What focus area(s) would you like to have?
- What skills would you like to be able to use regularly?
- What day-to-day activities would you prefer?

Be a Realistic Optimist

Right now, you might not be feeling your most confident about much of anything. Remind yourself that this is only temporary. You have worked before, and you will work again.

It's important to be both realistic and optimistic as you manage these challenges. You have a wealth of work experience and skills to help you succeed in a new role. You also get to do something that you enjoy and that gives you a sense of purpose and fulfillment. Take this time to figure out the key characteristics of that job so you can make strides towards finding the next right job for you. Once you have that target role clearly in mind, you can take steps toward making that a reality.

A Note About Your Goals and Preferences Over Time

When I think of my career, I realize that the "right next job for me" has changed depending on the rest of my life.

I've never been a five-year plan person. However, I know that my chosen field of learning and development is the right one for me. Since I'm driven to help people, my work revolves around helping identify problems or opportunities at a company, figuring out how to do something well, and helping others learn that. Instead of approaching my career with a specific job title in mind, I've committed myself to continuous learning and being open to where my professional life might take me next.

Here is how figuring out the next job for me looked at different points in life:

- Early in my career, I found my way into a demanding software training position where I traveled weekly and worked constantly. I learned about training best practices, teaching adults, and using software. The work was all-consuming, and I loved my coworkers, what I was learning, and advancement opportunities. I remember being at my mom's July 4th picnic and having a family friend ask me what I did outside of work, and I could not think of one other thing I did. At that time, though, it was the right job for me.

- When I was the single parent of a toddler, I had a job where I managed interesting projects and had two knowledgeable coworkers to mentor me. I learned all about employee benefits and even got to travel occasionally. The more reasonable 40-hour work week, easy commute, supportive organization, interesting work, robust benefits package, and stable environment were what I needed. At that time, it was the right job for me.
- Once I was the parent of a high school sophomore, and my new husband had a more flexible schedule, I took a more demanding training leadership role with a fast-paced technology company. I led a team of people, created training programs from the ground up, traveled, and worked in a high-growth fly-by-the-seat-of-my-pants environment. This challenging job had exciting new problems to solve. At that time, it was the right job for me.

Overall, what you want from paid work will change over time. Be sure to take the time to assess where you're at, what is working for you, and what you would like to change as you move forward. You get to choose the work situation that meets your needs and is the right job for you and where you are at in life.

Lesson Summary

To be successful in your job search, it's vital for you to do some soul searching about what you want from your career. Reflect on what you want to do when you grow up (your longer-term goals) and what you want to do next (your shorter-term goals).

Use this layoff as an unexpected opportunity for that reflection. Use these Structured Soul Searching activities to determine what you want and the kind of work that will make you happy. Make sure what you want to do next is aligned (or at least not contradictory) to what you want long-term. Learn about who you are and what matters to you. Reflect on your values, learn about your strengths, and consider what you liked and didn't like in your previous roles. Use what you learn as you think about the next right job for you.

In addition, think about the salary you want. Remember, there is more to compensation than just your base salary and more to any job than just the paycheck you'll earn. Identify those different salary-related numbers that matter to you. Arrive at a range you can share with potential employers that goes from the minimum salary you would happily accept to the salary you'd be really excited about.

Your Next Steps

- Visit **TheLayoffLady.com/SoulSearching** to access links to the structured soul searching resources referenced.
- Take time to reflect on who and what you want to be when you grow up.
- Think about what you might want to be next and how it aligns with your long-term goal.
- Identify and reflect on your values.
- Identify and reflect on your strengths.
- Think about your preferences for your next role and prioritize your wants and needs.
- Identify your target salary range and prioritize the importance of other benefits.

Lesson Four: Shape and share your story.

My Disjointed Story

After layoff number seven, I put on my hiring manager hat and looked honestly at my resume. The truth was that an employer might have a few concerns about Candidate Brenda, including the following:

- This candidate is mid-career but was only at each of her last three positions for just under a year and a half. Does she get bored? Does she have a short attention span? Did she do something to have her role end? Did she actually get fired, and they let her resign? What's going on there?
- This candidate has been laid off from every job listed on her resume. How is that even possible? What is wrong with her? What are the odds of that happening to someone?
- This candidate's most recent position was a huge step backward in her career. Why did she go from a leadership position to an individual contributor role? Was she failing in her leadership roles? Was she in over her head? Can she not hack it?

Ugh. I now had a resume that required some explanation. I had to figure out how to preemptively answer a few questions to help employers see the wisdom in considering me as a candidate. I had to figure out how to create a narrative that included the answers to these questions:

- Why did you leave those previous positions?
- Why were you in those roles for such a short period of time?
- How did you manage to get laid off so many times?
- Why did you go from a director-level position to an individual contributor role?
- If we hire you for this role, will you be happy and stay?

Overall, I needed to address the real overarching question: "Is it worth the risk for us to hire you?"

I had to find a way to make those disjointed details into a coherent story that made my professional life make sense. I needed to learn how to shape and share the story of my career—past, present, and future. To ensure my job search success, I would have to learn how to tell my professional story so a hiring manager would see that I was a strong candidate for their opening.

After figuring out that I wanted to pursue a learning and development manager position, I crafted my answer to the "Tell Me About Yourself" interview question:

My name is Brenda Peterson, and since forever, I've been in the field of learning and development. In fact, three of my last four positions have been training leadership roles within fast-paced technology companies closer to the startup space. My last role, and several of my previous roles, ended in layoffs due to organizational changes and economic factors.

My most recent role was as an individual contributor with a finance company. While I learned a great deal, now I'm interested in stepping back into a manager role where I can lead a team and design learning experiences. I'm excited to find out more about this Learning and Development Manager role and how my training and organizational development skills can help your organization succeed long term.

Shape and Share Your Story

Now that you've determined what you want in your next role, your next challenge is learning to tell your story. First, you need to tell the overall story of who you are professionally, the characteristics of roles that would be a good fit for you, and the value you bring. This includes proactively addressing any areas that may look like red flags to a potential employer.

Next, as you research and apply for jobs, you need to create a customized narrative for each job application you submit. As you continue to shape and share your story, you are making it easier for the hiring team to connect the dots between your skillset and the available role with their organization. You need to do your part to help a potential employer see how having your story continue with them is a logical course of action.

To this end, you'll use a few documents to summarize what you do, highlight your core accomplishments, and persuade that employer to learn more about you and how you could be a valuable addition to their company.

Be a Realistic Optimist

Coming into this job search, you've lived your life, and now you will apply for a job to work with different people, all of whom have had their own paths. You don't need to be perfect—and no job will be perfect either. You do, however, need to do your level best to position yourself and your strengths in a way that will help a potential employer see the value you bring. While not every employer will think you are the right fit for a given role, some will. In addition, sometimes you may apply for a position and then discover that it is not a good fit for you. Remember, your job is to present yourself well, help employers see your value, and know that not every job opportunity will work out for one reason or another.

Also know that you can only control what you do. No matter how well you shape and share your story, it won't resonate with every hiring team. This is why you'll continue to submit applications to multiple roles with various employers. Keep on doing those right things, and a role that is the right job for you will come to fruition.

Your Job Search Toolkit Helps You Share Your Story

Your job search toolkit is the collection of information you need to showcase your value to a potential employer. This includes your previous work experience, your skillset, your personality, how you get the job done, and your problem-solving ability. Let's look at the messaging, profiles, and specific documents that employers will request. Each helps you share a part of your story during the hiring process.

The What and Why of Your Job Search Toolkit

Here are the main pieces of your job search tool kit and the value of each item:

- **Your job search messaging:** Your job search messaging is the connective tissue that helps you talk about your skill set, your personal value proposition, and what you're looking for to help you advance your job search. You'll create messaging and use it in multiple places, including your LinkedIn profile, resume, social media posts, interview answers, and written communications. These are the critical components of your story that you'll share in many ways during your overall job search process.
- **Your LinkedIn profile:** LinkedIn is your professional billboard to the working world. It is an all-purpose marketing tool where people can view information beyond your resume, see which other people and companies you may have in common, and read the content you share in your posts. In addition, recruiters and hiring managers may contact you based on information included in your profile.
- **Your resume:** Your resume is the main document employers want to see when you submit a job application. This document needs to summarize who you are as a candidate as well as your most relevant skills, work history, education, professional affiliations, and accomplishments. This is also the stand-alone document that markets you as a desirable candidate for the available role.
- **Your cover letter:** Your cover letter introduces you to an organization and can include information to introduce or supplement your resume as needed. While not always required, if a company requests a cover letter, consider including one as a part of your application.
- **Your work samples:** Your work samples, often called your portfolio, are a way to demonstrate the skills you mention in your resume or LinkedIn profile. These work samples should give the hiring team an idea of your process and examples of your finished product. Depending on the type of work you do, a portfolio may not be needed.
- **Your references:** Your references are three people who are willing to vouch for you and the quality of your work. Having a list of these people and their contact information ready to go is helpful if and when ompanies request those details.

- **A tracking method:** Whether it's a spreadsheet, online document, or even a hand-written list, it's helpful to have a tracking method for record-keeping purposes. This list will help you monitor your applications, note your progress, and plan your follow-up on individual roles. While this may not feel like a part of telling your story, it definitely helps you keep your story straight as you talk with multiple employers.

Your Job Search Prework: Your Backstory

If an opportunity comes to you, it is to your advantage to be ready to pursue that job. Doing a little extra information gathering ahead of time will help you fill out a detailed job application, include a particularly relevant class, or remind a previous coworker of when you worked at that company together. Since time may be of the essence when applying, this will help you meet that tight deadline with fewer headaches.

Your Work History

When filling out job applications, having a thorough list of where you worked and basic information about each job can come in handy. Depending on the application, you may be able to submit a resume alone and be done with it. Other companies may ask you for specific start and end dates for each role. They may even ask for contact information for your immediate manager and the organization itself.

To make filling out more thorough job applications a little easier, I suggest you create a spreadsheet including information for your previous workplaces for the past 10-15 years. Depending on what stage you are at in your career, decide how many years of work experience it makes sense for you to gather.

Make sure to compile this information for each role:

- Company name.
- Company city and state.

- Job title.
- Start date.
- End date.
- Direct manager name.
- Reason for leaving.
- Your starting and ending salaries (for your information only).

While you're busy gathering information, you may want to note these items as well:

- Company phone number.
- Company street address.
- Additional company details: revenue numbers, employee count, and ownership structure.

Your Education and Professional Development History

Employers like to have assurances that a given candidate really has the knowledge, skills, and abilities they claim to have. This is why it's helpful to list the classes you've taken, groups you've joined, certification tests you've passed, and degrees you've completed. Having this type of external validation for your skill set adds to your credibility.

To customize your resume and make filling out a detailed job application easier, I suggest you create a spreadsheet to list the formalized ways you continue learning and growing.

I list my college degrees, Association of Talent Development (ATD) membership, a business analysis class I took, a vendor-specific train-the-trainer course I attended, and a few technical certifications.

Here are the core details to gather on each line item:

- Company/school.
- Course or certification date.
- Graduation/completion date.
- Membership start and end dates (if applicable).

- Expiration date (if applicable).
- Notes.

Keep in mind that this list is intended to accommodate everything from a 1-hour seminar you took once upon a time on sales prospecting all the way to an advanced degree. You may want to make separate lists for different activity types. Use the format that works best for you.

Your Job Search Messaging: The Story of You and Your Next Job

Your overall job search messaging helps you showcase who you are, your qualifications, and how you can add value to a given organization. This messaging can be repurposed anytime you want to communicate with a new person about your job search, a specific role of interest, or a company that seems like a good fit. This messaging will help you share the story of who you are, what you bring to the table, and what you want in your next role.

Messaging Guiding Principles

To begin, let's look at guiding principles for how to approach job search messaging:

- Be mindful of your goals.
- Stay positive.
- Customize your message for your audience.
- Build rapport.
- Add value.
- Be specific.
- Keep your asks small.

What You Want

In the previous chapter, you thought about the characteristics of your target job. Now, it's time to take that information and make it into a clear statement outlining what you want in your next role.

Be sure to include the following details:

- Your target job title.
- Working arrangements: hours per week, job location, remote/onsite/hybrid.
- Company size and industry.
- Skills you want to use.
- The type of work you want to do, including the problems you want to help solve.

Here are two examples of how this could look:

- I'm seeking a full-time technical writer role with a software startup company. I want to work independently to document new and existing product functionality and optimize knowledge base searchability.
- I'm interested in finding a contract social media marketing consultant role where I can help a small to mid-sized business create their social media presence from the ground up. I want to develop and execute a business strategy to grow their audience size and engagement for video-focused platforms.

Writing a clear and concise "What I Want Statement" can help you as you review job openings you encounter and empower you to prioritize your applications to those that most closely align with your goals. You can also include a version of this statement in the following contexts:

- Your cover letter.
- Your LinkedIn About section.
- Emails to recruiters, connections, or hiring managers inquiring about roles.
- Social media posts asking for assistance in finding a new job.

Who You Are Professionally

In addition to your "What I Want" statement, you also need to be able to tell your career story clearly and concisely. Your professional summary is that paragraph of quick-hit information that starts to outline who you are, your qualifications, and what you bring to the table as a candidate.

Here are details to include in your professional summary:

- Who you are professionally.
- The type of work you do.
- What motivates you.
- Job titles that might be appropriate for you.
- Relevant skills.
- Areas of expertise.
- Talents and strengths.
- How you show up in the workplace.

Here are two examples of how this could look:

- Collaborative director of training who thrives when implementing best-in-class learning strategies. Experience building training programs from the ground up in fast-paced technology startups. Able to think strategically and execute tactically while managing ambiguity. Committed to continuous improvement and delivering scalable L&D programs that drive growth.
- Corrections officer with a background in state and county facilities. Able to maintain custody and control of inmates while creating a secure environment. Skilled in inmate supervision, diffusing conflicts, and enforcing policies consistently. Experience teaching classes on CPR and first aid.

Writing a clear and concise Professional Summary can be used in the following contexts:

- A starting point for introducing yourself to new people when they ask about your work.
- A starting point for your "Tell me about yourself" answer.

- A starting point for the Professional Summary section of your resume.
- A paragraph in your cover letter.
- A paragraph in your LinkedIn About section.
- A paragraph in emails to recruiters, connections, or hiring managers.

Your LinkedIn Profile: Your Professional Story

While your resume is a concise 1-2 page marketing piece intended to showcase your skills as they apply to a specific job, LinkedIn is your professional billboard to the whole working world.

When you apply for a job, you'll include your LinkedIn profile on your resume and expect hiring managers and recruiters to visit your profile to find out more about you. Recruiters may source you (invite you to apply or interview for an opportunity) based on the content of your LinkedIn profile. Having a LinkedIn profile is also a great place to connect with and stay in touch with previous coworkers, professional colleagues of all kinds, and people you meet in passing.

Here is my short list of LinkedIn dos and don'ts:

- **Headline:** Your headline is high-value space. I suggest you customize it instead of using the default text, usually your most recent job title and employer. Consider including your target job title first, then including additional keywords (like skills, focus areas, and your field). When you comment on someone's post, they will see your name and the first part of your headline. This field is searchable and may help recruiters find you.
- **About section:** The About section lets you tell your story. Use your Professional Summary text and/or a version of your Tell Me About Yourself answer as a starting point. You also have room to add additional bullet points if you would like to do so. Write this in the first person (using "I" language) and further showcase who you are professionally.
- **Public profile URL:** By default, your LinkedIn profile's URL (web address) will be long and not very meaningful. You can customize your URL to make it friendly; I suggest using some version of your name.

This will look more professional on your resume—and make your profile easier to find. Use your favorite search engine to learn how to customize your LinkedIn profile URL.

Many job seekers are interested in optimizing their LinkedIn profiles to ensure they get attention from recruiters and get their information in front of as many people as possible. I encourage you to use your favorite search engine to learn more about the most current iteration of the LinkedIn algorithm. This will help you understand what is driving LinkedIn search results so you can take steps to make your profile show up more often. This may include updating common industry words in your headline, adding to your descriptions of your previous roles, or modifying the frequency and content of your posts.

For the current best practices on setting up and optimizing your LinkedIn profile, use your favorite search engine to find "LinkedIn Profile Best Practices" and the current year. You can also check out my blog at **TheLayoffLady.com** for my ongoing insights on all things LinkedIn.

You may notice that I haven't touched on the idea of networking on LinkedIn. Right now, we're doing the foundational work of building out your profile to maximize impact. We'll dive into the whys and hows of professional networking a little later on.

Your Job Application Materials: The Story of Your Future in this Role

Now, let's get into the actual materials you may be asked to submit when applying for a job.

Your Resume

Previously, you thought about your answer to the question, "What do you want to be next?" You should have one or a handful of job titles that you will target during your job search. Select the job title most aligned to the roles that interest you most. We'll use that job title and associated skills to create a resume that you will use as a starting point for each position for which you apply.

In a recent job search, the title I targeted was Learning Consultant. I included a good selection of applicable keywords and stories demonstrating a wide range of skills. This way, each time I applied for a specific job, I had my resume already 80-90% done. For each application, I would customize terminology to align the way I talked about myself even more closely with the words included in the job description. This enabled me to customize a resume quickly and efficiently for each role.

Resume Best Practices

As a many-time hiring manager, I have also seen a lot of bad resumes, many sort-of-okay resumes, and just a few that I would call good. Based on my observations of what works and what doesn't, here are my recommendations for writing a solid resume:

1. **Include basic information:** At the top of your resume, include your first and last name, email address, phone number, city, state, and LinkedIn URL.
2. **Use headings to organize content.** Include the following sections on your resume: Professional Summary, Work Experience, Education, and Professional Development. Consider including a Relevant Skills section to highlight in-demand skills.
3. **Use a chronological resume.** Include your work history with descriptions and list your most recent jobs first.
4. **Start with a professional summary section.** Give the resume reviewer a three to four-line overview of who you are and the value you bring to the role.
5. **Keep it to one or two pages.** Regardless of the length of your work and educational history, you get up to two pages to convey your value. Not six. For goodness sake, not 20. Two. Prioritize accordingly.
6. **Keep it recent.** Focus on your last 10-15 years of work experience.
7. **Include relevant keywords.** Review multiple job descriptions and include the language employers typically use to describe what to do.

8. **Show results.** When describing your work activities, include the results you achieved whenever possible. Describe and quantify how you saved time, reduced costs, increased efficiency, and boosted productivity.

9. **Don't get fancy.** Many resume formats include pictures, charts, columns, diagrams, and more. Excessive formatting may make it hard for an ATS (Application Tracking System) to read them properly. Keep your design straightforward and clean.

10. **Skip some details.** Include only information that adds value. Leave off a picture of yourself, cutesy graphics, your home address, contact information for previous supervisors, education-related dates, and "references available upon request." This will help you optimize your content, focus on your recent work experience, and minimize initial assumptions people might make about your age.

Your Cover Letter

If an employer asks for a cover letter, I include one. A cover letter is intended to introduce and frame your resume and should be no more than one page. I format my cover letter with the same type of heading and formatting as my resume so my documents all have a consistent look and feel. In some cases, if I'm submitting my resume via email, I will include an abbreviated version of my cover letter in the body of the email text.

Here is the basic cover letter format I use:

Date: Today's date

Greeting: Dear [Recruiting Team] or [Hiring Manager Name]

Paragraph 1: Please consider me for the [job title] role with [company]. I heard about this opening from [the person at your company who referred me or the website where I found this opening]. Because of [things I'm good at], I am interested to see how my skill set could make a strong contribution at [company].

Paragraph 2: [Repurpose your professional summary from your resume into first person, aka I am a...] End with a sentence like "I think my experience with [specific thing] makes me a strong candidate for this [job title] role with [company name].

Paragraph 3: I'm excited about this role. If you are interested in discussing this position and my qualifications, please contact me via email at [your email] or phone at [your phone number].

Closing: Sincerely, or Thanks! [Your first and last name, phone number, email, and LinkedIn URL]

For additional options for writing cover letters, consult your favorite search engine and find a format that feels right for you—and get ready to read about a lot of people hating on cover letters.

Your Work Samples

Depending on your chosen profession, you may be asked to share samples of your work. Having work samples available can help expedite the hiring process. Some roles may even ask for a link to your online portfolio during the application process and only consider you as a candidate if you have one available.

Since I work in learning and development, much of my work revolves around putting together training programs, creating handouts, producing videos, writing documentation, and delivering classes in person or via webinar. I expect to be asked for work samples as a part of my hiring process. This could be as formal as an early request to submit a URL for my online portfolio or as impromptu as someone asking during an interview, "Do you have any work samples you could take me through?"

When creating a portfolio, start by determining the type of work you want to showcase. A marketing specialist might include samples of a campaign calendar they designed and a newsletter they published. A website designer might include links to web pages they created and customer testimonials. An eLearning developer might include examples of videos and eLearning modules they developed. I suggest following thought leaders in your industry on LinkedIn and finding out more about what they recommend including in your portfolio.

Many people use an online drive to house their samples or have a dedicated webpage. I suggest using your favorite search engine to find best practices for what to include in your portfolio and how to present your work samples well for your industry.

Your References

Occasionally, companies will ask for your references either during the application process or when it looks like they may make you a job offer. Your professional references should be people who can attest to your work style, quality, and knowledge. I prefer to include one person I reported to, one coworker I worked alongside, and one I managed. Do what feels right for you.

Just in case I need it, I have a separate Professional References document and include the following details for each of my references:

- First and last name.
- LinkedIn URL.
- Their preferred email address.
- Their preferred phone number.
- A sentence about our professional relationship.

I format my references document like my resume so my documents all have a consistent look and feel.

Before I share my references' contact information with anyone, I ask each reference if they are open to discussing our experiences working together with potential employers. In addition, I contact my references to let them know each time I share their contact information with a potential employer. As someone who has been blindsided by getting a reference call for a former coworker whom I barely remembered, I beg of you–don't put your references in that position. I usually send a heads-up message like this:

Hi, [Reference name]. Thank you for agreeing to be one of my references. I recently applied for an Account Manager Role with ZYX Company. As a reminder, you and I worked as Sales Development Representatives for LMNOP Corp from 2016 to 2019. Please let me know if you hear from them!

Notice I also reminded them of when we worked together and our titles. I suggest you do what you can to make it easy for them to give you a good reference—and be willing to return the favor as needed.

Your Job Tracker

Be sure to track at least a few details on your job applications. Keeping this information will help you see what is working, what is not, and which roles need follow-up.

Whether you use whatever fancy online tools the cool kids are using these days or some other method, I suggest you track these details:

- **Application date:** The date you formally submitted your application.
- **Job title:** As listed in the job description.
- **Employer:** The name of the employer.
- **Referrer:** If someone referred you for a role, note who.
- **Job description link:** Consider saving an actual copy of the job description, too.
- **Application status:** Descriptors may include applied, interviewing, offer, rejected, etc.
- **Last action:** Descriptors may include applied, interview scheduled, thank you note sent, etc.
- **Salary range:** Include what the employer shared and what you told them.

Your tracking can be as lowbrow or high-end as you like. The goal of this is to help you keep track of each job and where you stand in the hiring process. Track whatever helps you achieve your goals.

You are the CEO of You

As the CEO of You, promote yourself well but truthfully. Just like companies get in trouble when they misrepresent themselves or their accomplishments, accurately share your credentials and qualifications. However, you should also position yourself positively and highlight your strengths, value, and achievements. This all comes down to your professional reputation, which can positively or negatively impact your future employability.

You Interview Answers: Story of You and Your Accomplishments

Once you have moved from applying to interviewing, you need to be ready to talk about yourself. Fortunately, since you've updated your resume and LinkedIn profile and have the job description from the specific position, you have a good starting point for preparation. Let's look at tried and true strategies for interacting with interviewers.

Answering Frequently Asked Interview Questions

Much of the job search involves you answering questions about yourself, your qualifications, and your possible fit for an available role.

These frequently asked interview questions typically come early on. This might be in the very first phone screen interview with a recruiter or at the beginning of any conversations you have with a new person. That could be the hiring manager, potential coworkers, or another company leader.

Here are the core interview questions I recommend you are able to answer:

Tell me about yourself.

This is the biggest frequent flyer of all the interview questions—and one that many people answer poorly. This is your opportunity to set the tone for the interview and shape the conversation. Use this time to briefly summarize your relevant professional history, highlight your most important qualifications, and emphasize why you are interested in the role.

- **Bad answer:** Not much to tell.
- **Why it is bad:** You just missed a huge opportunity to promote yourself as a solid candidate for this job.
- **Another bad answer:** I'm 42 years old, happily married, have 4-year-old twins, love riding horses, and volunteer weekly at my synagogue.
- **Why it is bad:** This is a great way to introduce yourself to another parent at a school event. In a job interview, you should highlight the value you bring to this job. This answer also includes details that don't impact your ability to do this job and that employers can't ask due to discrimination-related laws.
- **Good answer:** I have ten years of experience in social media specialist roles with small community organizations. I'm excited about this position because I can use my content marketing and event promotion knowledge with a larger company who needs help running industry conferences. I look forward to discovering how my skill set could help me contribute strongly to this role.
- **Why it is good:** This is an excellent example of highlighting interview appropriate information quickly and concisely.
- **Another good answer:** I'm an experienced social media specialist who loves promoting small community organizations. What excites me, though, is getting into promoting events and industry conferences–which I know is a focus for this role. When I saw this opening at XYZ Company, I asked my friend Alice, who is on the sales team, and she told me it was a great place to work. I'm excited to discuss my experience and what I could bring to this new role.
- **Why it is good:** This answer showcases your skills AND lets the interviewer know you did your homework.

Why are you looking for a new job?

Companies are interested in why you want to make a change. They may also be leery if they perceive that you have made too many changes within a short period of time. In addition, they might just want to see if you badmouth your previous/current employer or if you're respectful. Overall, be truthful, stay positive, and keep it short.

The question: Why are you looking for a new role? Why did you leave your last job?

- **Bad answer:** My last company was a financial nightmare, and I got fired.
  Why it is bad: Trashing your last company or manager reflects poorly on you. Tell the truth, but do so in a short, neutral way.
- **Another bad answer:** My last job was stupid and my boss laid me off because he hated me.
  Why it is bad: Again, talking trash=bad, and insults are even worse.
- **Good answer:** I'm looking for a role with additional growth opportunities.
  Why it is good: This answer is a great way to show that you are focused on moving forward.
- **Another good answer:** I was laid off earlier this year, and this role looks like a great fit for me.
  Why it is good: This is a nice short answer on why you're job searching and a quick positive reason why you applied for this one.

What do you know about our company?

Employers want to know that you've done your homework and know at least a little bit about your possible future employer.

The question: What do you know about our organization?

- **Bad answer:** Which job is this again?
  Why it is bad: Not remembering who you're talking to is a terrible start.
- **Another bad answer:** Not a thing.
  Why it is bad: Be able to state a few basic facts from the company's website.
- **Good answer:** XYZ Loans is a mortgage company focusing on VA and FHA loans. I see you recently rolled out a new veteran appreciation program and hired a new VP of Veteran Relations and that you just received an award for your charity work with DAV.
  Why it is good: Use your favorite search engine to find out some basics about the company. Mentioning what they are known for or a recent award shows you care enough to do some research.

- **Another good answer:** I know ABC Manufacturing just acquired CBA Manufacturing. This makes you the second-largest company making and selling biodegradable cups in the Midwest. I also know that my friend and former coworker, Kay, really enjoys being a part of the Women in Manufacturing group you started three years ago. **Why it is good:** Knowing current news about a company or mentioning that you know someone who works there and likes it helps build your tie to the organization.

Why are you interested in this role?

Companies often want to ensure you want the available position, not just any old job. Whether you have a straightforward career path or have bounced around a bit, companies may want to understand how the role you're applying for fits into your overall plan. This question also allows you to talk about who you are, what you know about the role, and the skills you bring.

What made you apply for this opening with our company?

- **Bad answer:** Which job is this again?
  Why it is bad: Not remembering the basics about this job means you're not coming back for the next round.
- **Another bad answer:** My current job is stupid and I hate my boss. **Why it is bad:** Reemphasizing yet again, trash talking=bad, and insults are even worse.
- **Good answer:** I learned a lot in my previous position as a project manager at XYZ Company, and this role as a Senior Project Manager with QRS Company seems like a good fit with my experience and career aspirations.
  Why it is good: Share why you want this role with this company and how it is a good next step for you.
- **Another good answer:** I saw that QWERTY Corp was named a top employer by our local newspaper. I'm excited to work for a company that has financial success and is highly rated by current employees.
  Why it is good: Again, share why you want this role with this company and how it is a good next step for you. Including a compliment is even better.

What does this role do?

Describing the role and core responsibilities is one way to show that you read the job description and understand what they are looking for. This may also help to show that you are interested in this job and haven't just been mass-applying.

The question: What is your current understanding of the core responsibilities in this job?

- **Bad answer:** Which job is this again?
  Why it is bad: This just hurts my soul.
- **Another bad answer:** I think, like, marketing maybe?
  Why it is bad: Better. But still terrible.
- **Good answer:** Based on the job description, the title is Sales Enablement Specialist. This role reports to the Sales Director and creates educational materials to support the account management team. This role also helps organize the annual in-person sales meeting event.
  Why it is good: Much better. You demonstrated that you read the job description and identified the essential points. Well done.
- **Another good answer:** So far, I understand that this Social Media Manager role sets the overall strategy for the company's LinkedIn presence. This person manages the Social Media Specialist role and has a dotted line to the VP of Customer Success. I've worked in this role in other organizations and have seen that partnering with the customer success team is a great way to align product marketing and customer engagement. I'd love to bring that to this role.
- **Why it is good:** Not only did you read the job description and comprehend it, but you also showed that you did a little extra research and highlighted why you would be great.

What is your desired salary?

While having salary ranges in job descriptions is becoming more common, it is not included in all job descriptions. Often, this question comes up in an application or as one of the final questions during an initial phone screen. Also, know that if it doesn't come up by the end of the second interview, you owe it to yourself to start that discussion to make sure the rate of pay works for you. The goal right now is to make sure that what you expect to make and what the company expects to pay are aligned enough that it's worth continuing the conversation. While it may feel awkward, it is better to know now that you're not aligned than to waste hours talking about a position that won't make either of you very happy.

The question: What are your salary requirements for this position?

- **Bad answer:** I have no idea.
  Why it is bad: It's important to think about what you want in a salary. I suggest using techniques discussed earlier in this book. At the very least, say it's "negotiable." It's still not great, but it's better than having zero clues.
- **Another bad answer:** A very low salary.
  Why it is bad: Make sure you have an idea of what jobs like this pay and what the typical value is. Don't sell yourself short. Including a very low number may cause the company to doubt your skill level.

- **Good answer:** What is the salary range for this position?
  Why it is good: I think this is the best answer to the question. Ask this question to answer their question—and follow their response up with your commentary about where you fit into that range.
- **Another good answer:** My general salary range is [low end of your range] to [high end of your range]. I'd like to revisit this topic as I learn more about the position, including bonuses and benefits.
  Why it is good: On rare occasion, the interviewer will not answer my counter-question of "What is the salary range." In these cases, I suggest you give them a range and manage expectations that you'll revisit this conversation as you learn more about the role.

What questions do you have for me?

This is your opportunity to ask questions. Given that you have a job description and not much else about this role at this point, take this opportunity. I suggest asking two questions about the role itself and a final question about the next steps in the hiring process.

The question: Do you have any questions for me?

- **Bad answer:** Nope.
  Why it is bad: Asking at least one question shows you are engaged and genuinely interested.
- **Another bad answer:** How much time off do I get? How soon can I take time off?
  Why it is bad: This early in the process, I ask about the position, not just when and how often they will pay you for the days you don't have to work in the job you do not yet have.
- **Good questions to ask:** Ask questions to find out valuable information about the role, the company, your interviewer, and the next steps in the hiring process.

- What are the first projects this position would tackle?
- What are the markers of success for this job?
- What does the onboarding process look like?
- Tell me about the company culture.
- What brought you to this company?
- What keeps you at this company? What do you like about working here?

- What are the next steps in the hiring process?
- What does the overall interview process look like?

Answering Behavioral Interview Questions

Behavioral interview questions often begin with the phrase, "Tell me about a time" and require you to mine your personal experience and answer by telling a story related to your responsibilities and accomplishments from your previous jobs.

Finding Your Stories

When answering these types of questions, you will tell a story. It's valuable to think about your previous work experience and be ready to mine that experience for stories to highlight your qualifications to your interviewers. Your goal should be to give a one to three-minute answer that showcases your skills in ways that address the question.

The tendency is for people to either not know what to say or to ramble and hope they stumble upon something useful. We'll explore a more structured approach to answer this question:

Tell me about a time when you had to finish a project with a short turnaround time.

Answering With No Plan

Gosh. I've done a lot of projects where I had to get something done quickly. Those have included software implementations, making a video, and even designing or updating a class with little to no notice. I usually just work really hard and put in extra hours to get something done. I'm a really hard worker.

So one case I can think of was when my company decided to do less travel to save money and be more efficient. I worked for a software company that delivered most of its training in person at customer sites. Because it took one person out of the training rotation for a week at a time, and they couldn't do anything with other customers, we knew we had to figure out a way to do it right away. It was also getting close to the end of the quarter, so my manager wanted a proposal to give to his boss showing how we understood that it was a big issue and that we would solve it right away. We had to figure out how to deliver what was usually four days of in-person training without traveling to a customer site. We really didn't know how we were going to pull that off.

We had to figure out how to do that well—and we had to figure it out in about a week. We didn't have to start doing it that next week, but we had to have a plan to share within the organization. A few of us—including a salesperson, a trainer, and an instructional designer—sat down and tried to figure out what to do. We didn't want to bore people to death with webinars that were way too long and make it an awful experience. It was really hard to figure out.

[So far, there has been a lot of talking, and we are still just setting the stage.]

CARL: Context, Action, Results, Learning

There are a few popular models for answering interview questions. You may have heard of STAR or PAR. I prefer the CARL method. Here's what each component addresses:

- **Context:** Set the scene for the story you are telling and the problem you were trying to solve. What company did you work for? What was their focus? What was the problem? Why did the problem matter?
- **Action**: Describe what you did. What did you think about first? What actions did you take? What specifically did you do? Why did you choose that course of action over others? Who did what?
- **Results**: Explain the result. What tangibly happened? Was the customer happier? Did the problem go away? What were the short-term impacts? How did this work out in the long run? What did you gain? Did you avert a loss?
- **Learning**: What did you learn? Did you continue to do this? Did you come up with another, better option later? Did you learn something about yourself?

A CARL Answer

- **Context:** My department was responsible for training new customers on our software, and we did that through in-person training at the customer's site. Because this solution was costly, and each trainer could only train one customer per week, my manager wanted to find a more efficient solution to reduce costs and increase instructor utilization. We also needed a plan to present to the VP the following week.
- **Action:** I talked with multiple stakeholders, including leaders, salespeople, trainers, and even a couple of customers. I found out what

they each thought about the current solution, what they liked about our current practices, and their thoughts on alternatives. We created a pilot for a blended learning solution that combined virtual instructor-led training and self-paced hands-on practice. I build consensus among internal stakeholders on this solution.

- **Result:** As a result, I created a written plan outlining this blended learning solution and created a pitch deck for my boss to use with the VP. We proposed to pilot this plan in six weeks with a customer where we had a solid working relationship and who was adding another division. My boss presented the plan, and we moved forward with the pilot.
- **Learning:** This process taught us more about what was important to the VP and other stakeholders and alternative ways to deliver time and cost-efficient customer-facing training.

Lesson Summary

Knowing what you want is crucial in talking to employers about who you are, your priorities, and what value you bring. Use what you learned about yourself and your skills as you assemble job application materials like your resume, cover letter, and work samples.

Use your LinkedIn profile as your professional billboard to promote you as a candidate who can solve the problems employers need to address. Use your job search messaging to communicate with others about what you want in your next role and how they can help you.

When you leverage strategies to promote your professional value, interact with other people's content, and possibly even attract attention from recruiters looking for candidates like you. You'll also focus on doing those right things you need to do to succeed in your job search.

Your Next Steps

- Assemble your work history.
- Assemble your educational history.
- Write your "What I Want" statement.
- Write your professional summary.
- Update your LinkedIn profile.
- Create your job-specific resume.
- Create your basic cover letter format.
- Gather and determine how to share your work samples with prospective employers.
- Identify your references and list their contact information.
- Determine how you will track your job search progress.
- Write out your answers to commonly asked interview questions.
- Identify stories that you will use to answer behavioral interview questions.
- Use the CARL format to structure your answers to behavioral interview questions.

Lesson Five: Help people help you.

Asking My LinkedIn Network for Job Search Help

One week after my position was eliminated, I took a deep breath and made a post on LinkedIn asking for help from my professional network:

As of earlier this month, I am in a career transition. Now, I am looking to you, my LinkedIn network, for your help in finding my next opportunity!

I am seeking a full-time learning and development position, preferably remote, with up to 30% travel. I am interested in roles with larger organizations where I can be a strong contributor and leverage my skills in needs assessment, performance consulting, change management, instructional design, and learning facilitation.

Job titles that may be appropriate for me include Learning Consultant, Instructional Design Manager, Training Manager/Director, or Learning and Development Lead. I am open to roles as a strong individual contributor, managing the learning function, managing a team, or player/coach.

If you are aware of any open positions that might be a good fit or know any individuals or recruiters I should be talking with about possible opportunities, please let me know. I also ask you to like, share, or comment on this post to help me boost the signal. Thank you for your assistance and support in this process!

Over the next week, this post was viewed by 9,443 people, had 132 likes, and received 93 comments. It also led me to have 11 conversations with people I had not met previously. Each person shared their job search insights, let me know about open positions, and even connected me with their networking contacts who they knew could help. Three of those conversations led to interviews. A month and a half later, one of those interviews led to my new job.

Don't Go It Alone

Life is challenging when nothing out-of-the-ordinary is happening. It's even harder when you're going through an unexpected job change. While I'm a fan of self-reliance, I also know how important it is to find your people and support one another as you go through challenges. You're not weak for needing people. You are strong because you know the value of building and leveraging relationships to help get you through trying times.

Going through a layoff and the following job search is a lot to manage on your own. Be sure to remind yourself that you are not the first person to go through this. You have people who care about you, including your close friends, family, and even acquaintances. Let those people help you.

Help Them Help You

I have found that people genuinely want to help. In many cases, though, they might not know what you need. Not only is it vital that you seek out help when you need it, but you need to figure out what type of help you need from people.

This is also when you discover that many people don't know exactly what it is you do for a living. Instead of being taken aback that they don't know, use this as an opportunity to figure out how to tell them what you want and need. By including job titles, industries, and types of companies, you give them a fighting chance of being able to help you.

You are the CEO of You

When you're the CEO of a company, you're not expected to know everything about everything. Instead, you have a board of directors and advisory employees who advise you and help you make better decisions. In the end, you're accountable for those choices.

The same is true in your role as the CEO of You. Rely on different people to help you in the various aspects of this project. Going it alone is not admirable—it's a missed opportunity. Leverage those people for the help you need and commit to being a good corporate partner of theirs going forward.

Building Your Career Transition Support Team

It takes a village to get you through a career transition. Relying on one person for everything is all kinds of stressful—for you and them. Overall, people generally want to help, and you need to let them. It's a matter of figuring out what you need and connecting with individuals depending on your specific need at that time.

Here's a starter list of the types of personal help you might need:

- **Emotional support**: You'll have all the feelings. Figure out who you can talk to about what. Sometimes you'll laugh, sometimes you'll cry, sometimes you'll vent, and at your worst, maybe all of the above.
- **Communication**: The simple act of telling people the news about your unplanned job change can be draining. Your news may also result in people inadvertently trying to allay their own job loss fears by talking about them to you. Instead, find a friend who can help you spread the word.
- **Sounding board:** When considering a big decision or trying something new, running it past another person helps. You may not even need your sounding board people to say much, just to listen. Ask those trusted people to help you think through ideas as you choose your next steps.
- **Logistical support:** Sometimes, you'll need a hand figuring out how to make something work. Maybe it is having someone watch your child during a phone interview, using a neighbor's printer, or finding a ride to an interview. Let people help you solve a problem at a time when you may be struggling with figuring out one more thing.
- **Fun:** There will be many times when you just need a distraction. It may be taking a walk, grabbing a coffee, or watching a movie. Enjoy a good chat about nothing—and not having to be your interview-ready self.
- **Cheerleader:** Sometimes, you'll just need a pep talk. Encouragement is

vital whether it's someone sending you a quick "You've got this!" text or a reminder to take a deep breath and tell your interviewer your amazing story about solving that big work problem.

In addition, here are a few examples of the kind of help you might need as it relates to your job search:

- **Accountability:** You may need someone to help you follow through on tasks. It may be as easy as them asking if you applied for a job you mentioned or following up to see if you updated your resume as planned. Texting someone after you complete a task is an excellent way to stay on track.
- **Professional feedback:** Whether you talk with someone who works in a particular industry, a hiring manager, or a resume writer, figuring out how to be a more effective job searcher is useful. Tap into those people who can give you feedback as you move through your process.
- **Connectors:** We have people in our personal and professional networks who seem to know everybody. Let them help you connect with people, job leads, or ideas when you need them. Sometimes, asking them questions like "Do you know anyone who would be willing to chat with me about [specific topic]?" can help you make headway toward your career goals.

Your Personal and Professional Networks

Of all the types of help you'll need, many areas listed above are personal. Remember, you need to take care of yourself and your core needs so you have the energy and momentum to focus on your job search. From that list of types of help you may need, many of those will be fulfilled by your personal network—those friends and family who are there for you during difficult times.

Networking just means meeting people. That's all. When we were kids, that was called "making friends," and we learned to do it without really trying. If you sat next to someone in your science class and talked regularly, you were friends. If you usually shared a seat with someone on the bus, you were friends. If you played on the same 4-H softball team, you were friends. Making friends was just a thing we did with the people we were around all the time.

As a working adult, professional networking is simply making more friends who have business-related things in common. With the prevalence of social media, we added different kinds of relationship labels.

When I think of my Facebook network, I think of my friends list. My Facebook friends are predominantly friends and family sharing information about our personal lives—like pet videos, family photos, and vacation news, with occasional mentions of work (and occasional fits and spurts of politics here and there).

Conversely, when I think of my LinkedIn network, I think of my professional connections and the focus on job changes, photos from business conferences, asking for advice on business challenges, and sharing articles on industry best practices with occasional mentions of their personal lives work (and occasional fits and spurts of politics here and there). When I'm job searching, my LinkedIn network connects me with potential job opportunities to help me find a role that leverages my skill set.

We'll spend most of this chapter on work relationships and how to create, nurture, and grow your professional network by leveraging LinkedIn.

About LinkedIn

Professional networking is the total of my interactions with people professionally. Meeting and getting to know people takes place in multiple ways—including in-person meetings, emails, phone calls, Zoom meetings, and more.

LinkedIn is not my professional network. LinkedIn is, however, a social media platform and a valuable tool that many people (including me) use to keep track of people who have a role in my work life. LinkedIn is, at its core, a way for me to keep track of all of those professional relationships, interact with people in a systematic way, and help each of us get more of what we need professionally to achieve our goals.

Like any website, technique, or theory, LinkedIn is not the magical answer to all your job search woes. Creating a LinkedIn account will not automatically get you hired. Some people do not use LinkedIn and manage to find and maintain gainful employment without it. LinkedIn is a tool that can help you reach more people during your job search. The amount of success you may have with LinkedIn hinges on you getting crystal clear on what you want, growing your professional network, and leveraging strategies to present yourself well and communicate effectively with others. Just like buying a treadmill and using it as a closet annex will not help you shed those unwanted pounds, creating a LinkedIn account that you never use (or misuse) will not make you employed.

In that long list of the types of support you need, while going through a career transition, we'll focus on using LinkedIn as it relates to your job search.

Mutually Beneficial Relationships

For a networking relationship to be a good one, it must be mutually beneficial. Each person should share valuable information and opportunities to help the other out. Make sure to balance your interactions with people to ensure you're providing value and not just taking. When someone helps you, thank them, and ask how you can help them, too.

Strategies for LinkedIn Connections

When I think about building my professional network, adding new LinkedIn connections is one of my markers of success. When you add a connection, you can see one another's posts and send messages to one another. I use LinkedIn to create, build, and maintain my professional relationships by adding people as connections.

Turning People You've Met into LinkedIn Connections

When I first started using LinkedIn, I only connected with people I had met in person. At that time, my network mainly included the following people:

- Family and friends.
- Current and former coworkers, colleagues, and business associates.
- People I met through introductions from my current professional connections.

Creating New Professional Connections

When the pandemic hit, I realized I needed to shift my approach, or I would not meet anyone new. I also realized that since more companies were open to hiring remote people, I needed to broaden my network beyond the people I would encounter in person. In addition, I now also proactively send connection requests to a wider variety of people, including the following:

- People in my geographical area.
- People in fields similar to mine, like learning and development, organizational development, sales enablement, and talent development.
- People who work at organizations that interest me.
- Recruiters.
- People with common interests or experiences.
- People with mutual connections.

Again, the more people I meet, and connect with who know my professional value, the better I will be able to find a new role that meets my requirements more quickly.

Personalizing Connection Requests

In most cases, I personalize a connection request when I send it. When connecting with people I've met in person, I always remind them of where we met, including details about our meeting, sharing helpful information, and an invitation to connect.

Personalizing the request becomes even more critical if I send a connection request to someone I have not met before.

I include the following components when personalizing a connection request:

- **Greeting:** Hi, [person's first name spelled correctly].
- **Personal note:** Include details on how you met, compliment them on a previous post, share a helpful tip, comment on their situation, or point out something we have in common.
- **Invitation to connect:** I'd like to add you to my professional network. Let's connect!
- **Signature:** [Your Name]

Here are a few examples of what I might include as a personal note in my personalized connection requests.

- I see that we both attended this morning's ATD-Nebraska webinar. I'm new to Omaha, and I'm excited to connect with L&D professionals in the area.
- Thanks for your recent post on tips for engagement in webinars. Now, I have a few new techniques to try!
- Sorry to hear about your recent layoff. I also have a background working in SaaS startups in the software space. Let me know if I can help you make connections during your job search.
- I'm also in the field of L&D focusing on technical training. Hearing how your team uses short-form videos to engage new employees was great.

Strategies for Following People and Companies on LinkedIn

In some cases, you may want to follow people on LinkedIn rather than connect. Following someone means you can now see their posts in your activity feed, but they do not see yours in their activity feed. This enables you to keep track of what they say and even comment on their posts. Sometimes,

I will start by following someone and interacting with their posts, and later invite them to connect.

In addition, I follow companies on LinkedIn as well. I follow my alma mater, companies in the field of L&D, companies where I'm applying for a role, community organizations, and professional development organization pages. This way, I can keep track of their posts and occasionally share them. When it comes to interviewing or talking to people about opportunities, being better informed about organizations and individuals helps make for more robust conversations.

Commenting on Posts

Once you have connected with someone, reading and commenting on their posts is an excellent way to build that relationship. This way, they are starting the conversation, and you are helping expand on that content and sharing your ideas. You can thank them for sharing ideas, adding your thoughts, sharing your experiences, and illustrating how you have used that concept. Commenting on posts also gives you an inroad to connect with someone else who is also interacting with that post. Commenting on existing posts is a great way to interact with others in your profession, build credibility, and make meaningful connections with people.

Strategies for Posting on LinkedIn

Sharing content on LinkedIn is a great way to engage with your connections, add value to your professional relationships, and promote who you are and what you know. Unfortunately, very few people ever post anything at all—which is a missed opportunity to differentiate yourself from others in your field.

When I've asked people what is stopping them from posting on LinkedIn, the overwhelming answer is, "I don't know what to post." Like with most everything in life, it comes down to your overall goals.

I post useful content to share knowledge and strengthen relationships while actively searching for jobs. There are many ways that posting on LinkedIn can help. In general, I suggest using LinkedIn to share who you are as a person and as a professional and demonstrate the value you bring.

LinkedIn Post Frequency

Another question that comes up is the frequency of posting. I recommend posting on LinkedIn no more than twice per day and posting one to four times per week. Use your favorite search engine for the latest recommendations on the best times and days of the week to post to get the most views on your posts.

LinkedIn Post Topics

What should you post about? Go back to your "what do I want to do next" information we covered earlier in this book. Look at the types of roles you want and the skills you want to promote. For me, working in Learning and Development, some of the skills I promote are instructional design, training needs assessment, learning retention, project management, and managing teams. While I browse LinkedIn, I often run across articles on these topics. I make a note of articles and resources and share them regularly.

LinkedIn Post Format

You don't have to write a lengthy, original manifesto to post on LinkedIn and make an impact.

Personally, most of the content I share on LinkedIn includes some version of the following:

- **Context:** A sentence or two framing the information I share and presenting its value.
- **Resource:** A link to an article, post, or eye-catching graphic.

- **Keywords:** I often include 2-4 hashtags to make my post more findable.

LinkedIn Post Ideas

Here are examples of what you can post on LinkedIn that will help you "build your brand" and share what you're all about, both professionally and as a person:

- **Showcasing your expertise:** Who are you professionally? What are your skills? What do you bring to the table as a possible company employee?I post about management skills, relationship building, instructional design, project management, facilitating classes, etc.
- **You as a person:** Who are you? What is it like to work with you? What are your interests? What do you care about? I occasionally post about board games, inline skating, my family, and coffee.
- **Inspirational content:** What picks you up when you are down? What insights struck you? What motivates you? I post quotes about learning, motivation, and being adaptable.
- **Promoting other people or organizations:** Who do you learn from?Who shared a useful resource that benefitted you? I post lessons learned and tag who I learned from.
- **You doing things:** What do you do? What did you write? How do you volunteer? I post about presenting webinars, my professional development activities, and working from coffee shops.
- **Your work samples:** What projects do you work on? What do you write? What content do you create? I post my blog articles and content from webinars I have attended.
- **Sharing opportunities and resources:** What problems can you help people solve? Who do you know who is a go-to person for a given topic? I post articles on adult learning and job search insights and tag people who share helpful information.

Job Search Assistance Post

When I have been laid off and am openly job searching, I have usually published a post to let my connections know that I am job searching and ask them for their assistance.

Writing Your Job Assistance Post

I include the following components when creating a job assistance post:

- **Quick summary of your situation:** When your job ended, your current status as being in career transition, asking your network for their help in your job search.
- **Brief note about your skills:** Include an introduction sentence like "Here are a few details about me" with 3-4 bulleted points on your unique skills.
- **Your target role:** Include an introduction sentence like "Here's what I'm looking for in my next role:" then specify the role you want. Include job location, work arrangements, and your target job titles.
- **Calls to action:** Include a sentence like "If you are aware of any open positions that might be a good fit for me (or know of any hiring managers or recruiters I should be talking with about possible opportunities), please share your thoughts in the comments or a message to me. I also ask that you like, share, or comment on this post to help me boost the signal.
- **Thank you:** Thank you for your assistance in this process!
- **A picture:** If you like, include a photo to attract attention and boost engagement.

Nurturing Your Job Assistance Post

Once you create your post, share a link to that post via LinkedIn messaging with your connections. For example, with my last job search, I sent individual messages to at least 100 of my connections asking them if they could visit that post, and then like, comment on, or repost it to help me jump-start my job search. I also commented and liked each comment received. Enlisting help from people already in my network helped me get this post in front of thousands of people. It helped generate job leads and burgeoning professional networking connections that helped me get closer to a new role.

Direct Messaging on LinkedIn

Like sending someone an email, you can also directly message your connections through LinkedIn Messaging. While most other communication methods via LinkedIn are one-to-many, this medium is one-to-one.

Messages That Add Value

When you contact people directly, be sure your messages are not all you asking others to do things for you. Here are a few types of messages you can send to your connections that add value to the relationship and give more than they take:

- Wishing them a happy holiday.
- Congratulating them on a promotion, job, degree, personal milestone, or accomplishment.
- Thanking them for sharing useful content that helped you personally.
- Thanking them for helping people in general.
- Checking in on them.
- Asking them to chat with someone who could benefit from their expertise.
- Telling them it was nice seeing them at an in-person or online event.
- Following up on a previous topic of conversation.
- Sharing a resource, article, or information that would help them.

Direct Asks for Help: Worst Practices

Asking for help is an art. First, you need to be willing to ask for help. Next, you need to craft your ask in a way that you have a higher likelihood of getting that help.

Here are the most significant issues I've seen with how people ask for job search help:

- Making a big ask early on.
- Making a vague ask.
- Making an ask that is disproportionate to how well you know someone.
- Making frequent asks.
- Being aggressive in asks.
- Re-asking too many times.
- Not being able to hear no.
- Being angry if you don't get what you want.

Even though I am, by nature, a helper, here are the types of requests I receive via LinkedIn messages that will not get much of a response from me.

- Can you get me a job at your company?
- Can you introduce me to people?
- If you hear of any openings, let me know.

Why are these not good asks? For one, these are big asks. These are also the types of requests that would require me to do a lot of investigation to be truly helpful. I'm not going to magically get you a job at my company. I'm also not going to go through my list of professional contacts, prioritize who I think you should meet, and facilitate multiple introductions. I will also not be your personal job searcher and send you roles—partly because there is no guarantee that my assumptions based on our past experience working together will align with your current job search goals. I'm also not willing to waste my time trying to read your mind or sending you irrelevant job listings.

When you ask people to help you, put in your work first. Then, when I know you are committed to being successful, I'm much more likely to help you clarify details.

Direct Asks for Help: Better Practices

Here are a few better asks, but may only work with connections who you know very well and who you have helped in the past:

- Would you review my resume?
- Would you review my LinkedIn profile?
- Would you recommend me for a position at your company?
- Would you pass my resume on to your connection, the hiring manager?
- Would you meet with me for 30 minutes to discuss [a professional topic]?

These requests are specific, which is better, but each is still a sizeable request. The first two may be time intensive. The next two involve me putting my reputation on the line to recommend you for a role. The one requires a block of my time on a yet-to-be-named topic. Depending on our interactions prior to these requests, my response may vary from "Of course!" to no response at all.

Direct Asks for Help: Best Practices

Asks are better when they are more specific and less unwieldy. It's also helpful if there is context. Here are a few questions that are more likely to get responses. The requests earlier in this list are most likely to get a response:

- I just made a job search post on LinkedIn. Would you be willing to visit the post [link here] and like, comment on, or share this post to help me boost my signal?
- I'm considering applying for the Associate Project Manager position with Super Cool Company. How do you like working there? Would you recommend it as a workplace?
- I am working on a career transition from being a software trainer to a project manager. What do you like about your current role as a project manager? What skills would help me in that role?
- I am working on a career transition from being a software trainer to a project manager. I see you're connected to Alonzo Johnson, a project

manager with Super Cool Company. Would you be willing to facilitate an introduction between us on LinkedIn?

- I'm considering applying for the Associate Project Manager position with Super Cool Company. As I get my application materials together, I'd appreciate your insights on the company and how to position myself for success. Would you be willing to have a 15-minute phone call sometime over the next week?
- I'm considering applying for the Associate Project Manager position with Super Cool Company. As I get my application materials together, I'd appreciate your insights on the company and how to position myself for success. Would you be willing to have a 30-minute virtual coffee meeting sometime over the next week?
- I'm considering applying for the Associate Project Manager position with Super Cool Company. As I get my application materials together, I'd appreciate your insights on the company and how to position myself for success. Would you be willing to meet for a coffee at the local coffee shop of your choosing? The first cup is on me!

Networking Meetings

A networking meeting is one way to build stronger relationships with one of your LinkedIn connections. A networking meeting is typically when you and another person decide to spend a half-hour-ish together. This meeting, sometimes called a coffee chat, could happen virtually or in person, often over coffee.

If you're job searching, the typical focus will be on how you can progress in your job search. Someone may agree to a networking meeting because you have things in common (like a field of work, background, professional goals), because they are generally committed to helping people when they are job searching, or because you have a mutual acquaintance to ask that person specifically to meet with you to help you out. Remember, your interactions with people will impact their desire to help you in the future.

Here are a few common types of networking meetings:

- Talking about a particular job opportunity with a specific   organization. Usually, the goal of that meeting is to gain insight from someone who works at that company to help you decide if the company sounds like a good fit, how to tailor your application to the organization, or even get a referral in.
- Talking about someone's career path to gain insight into what you might do to get into a specific job or field. In this case, you might ask someone about how they got into a specific role—like a manager, an instructional designer, or a digital marketer—to figure out what next steps you might want to take to get to a similar role.
- General job search career advice. In this case, the person you're meeting knows you are in a career transition and will help you determine your next steps. This could be them recommending job titles that you should look into, companies they know who are hiring, or people you might want to talk to to get closer to your goal of finding a job. Sometimes, this meeting might lead to the person saying, "I think you should talk to [SuperCool Person] who [can help you with an area where you need help].

The holy grail of networking meetings is when the person you meet with agrees to introduce you to someone else they know who could help you. That process repeats until you're talking to a hiring manager or influencer who can help you get an interview for a job. Having good networking meetings is a critical step in that process.

Asking For a Referral Directly

When applying for a job, having an employee referral improves your chances of being invited to interview. Many companies even do a financial incentive for candidates referred in by current employees. However, each person may have their comfort level with referring a candidate for a job.

Personally, I would not ask a brand new connection of mine for a referral. I know that I would not be comfortable referring someone I knew little about.

Cases Where I Think I'll Get a Referral

There are many people who I have directly asked to refer me for a job:

- Immediate coworkers.
- Connections who I have interacted with for years.
- People who have asked me to refer them in for a role.
- People who have referred me for a role in the past.
- People who I have had recent, strong interactions with.
- People who were laid off from the same company where I was laid off.

For these people, if I saw a job opening at a company where they worked, I would send this type of message, with additional personalization based on our familiarity:

Hi, [Person's name]. I'm wondering if you might be able to help me out.

I'm interested in applying for this job with [your company]. Would you be willing to refer me for the role? Sometimes, people get referral bonuses, so I wanted to check before applying. Let me know when you get a chance. Here is a link to the role I'm considering:

[Link to job posting]

Thanks!

–Brenda

Cases Where I Might Get a Referral

If it's someone I do not know as well, I may send a different message. This asks a more specific question and leaves the door open for them to offer to refer me if they are comfortable with that. In those cases, I might send a message more like this:

Hi, [Person's name]. How are you? It's been a bit since we [worked at x company/were in that group together/met at that Superbowl party].

I see you're currently working at XYZ company. I noticed they have an opening for a [Super Cool Job Title], and I'm considering applying. How do you like the organization? It's always nice to get an opinion from a current employee.

Let me know when you get a chance.

Thanks!

Out of this, I may get any of the following responses:

- No reply at all.
- This is an [awesome or awful] place to work.
- This is an [awesome or awful] place to work. You [should or should not] apply!
- This is an awesome place to work. I'm happy to refer you in and/or let me know when you apply so I can pass on your resume.

Be a Realistic Optimist

Remember, these people in your network, and many people you haven't even met yet, want to help you succeed. You're not putting them out by asking for help. You're fulfilling the fundamental need we all have to connect with others. Know that you might not get a referral from everyone, but you will find people who want to help you. Be that person who helps others in the future, too.

Also know that there will be people who you ask who will never respond to your request. Remember, not everyone will assist you when you ask. Regardless of the outcome, always be respectful and thankful for those willing and able to help.

Lesson Summary

Remember, it's important not to go it alone. Leverage your personal and professional networks to help you along the way. Nurture your network since networking relationships are not one-and-done but require ongoing touchpoints. Remember to reach out and leverage those relationships to help you navigate challenging feelings, talk through possible job search strategies and options, and even have fun along the way. Build your career support team and include people who can help you navigate all the emotions, help you along the way, and cheer you on when needed. Also include people who can help you professionally, from acting as a sounding board to resume review help to introducing you to others to interview prep. Let those people help you.

Re-tool your LinkedIn profile and your network to build your professional presence. Use LinkedIn to make new connections and follow business leaders and companies that interest you. Interact with people's posts and post helpful content. As you start building relationships, start by adding value before you start asking for favors. Use direct messages and make small, targeted asks while letting people know you want to help them. Overall, build long-term solid relationships by making those interactions mutually beneficial and collaborative.

Your Next Steps

- Identify who can help you in different ways during your career transition.
- Practice sending personalized connection requests.
- Strategically follow people and companies on LinkedIn.
- Interact with LinkedIn posts that help you showcase your expertise.
- Consider posting on LinkedIn to continue to highlight your unique skill set.
- Consider making a job search assistance post on LinkedIn.
- Use best practices for directly asking for job search help.
- Use networking meetings to build stronger working relationships.

Lesson Six: Examine your energy to take control of your time.

Revising Plans Due to Energy Shortage

I had a relatively interview-free week ahead of me. I decided to make some non-job searching plans. On Tuesday, I would go to my favorite coffee shop. Early Wednesday, I would go to a professional development meeting and catch up with colleagues. Thursday afternoon, I would visit the aquarium at the zoo. Friday morning, I would FINALLY go to the grown-ups-only skating session at the roller rink. Later that evening, I would FINALLY check out that board gaming group.

Granted, I wasn't making much new job-related progress, but it would be a nice break.

On **Monday** morning, I applied for my weekly unemployment benefits, interacted with people on LinkedIn, and applied for two jobs. That afternoon, two companies invited me to initial phone screens. I scheduled one for early Tuesday and another for Thursday at noon. I stayed home Monday afternoon and researched the company for the Tuesday interview. That night, I did some laundry and ran the dishwasher, so I felt like I had accomplished something tangible.

On **Tuesday** morning, after my interview, two different companies invited me to second interviews. I scheduled one for late afternoon Thursday and the other for Friday after lunch. I stayed home Tuesday afternoon to prepare for those mission-critical second interviews later in the week. I took a break and went outside to take a short walk and let my mind wander. That night, I knit part of a hat and listened to the Star Wars soundtrack. I also glared at the pile of mail I still needed to sort through.

On **Wednesday**, I didn't have the social energy to spare. I skipped the event and spent most of Wednesday writing and doing job interview prep at my favorite coffee shop. This gave me a much-needed change of scene where I didn't have to interact a lot with people. That night, I came home, hung out with my husband, and played a puzzle game on my phone. I put off sending post-interview thank-you notes because writing interesting sentences felt impossible.

On **Thursday** morning, going to the zoo seemed like more work than fun. Instead, I drank my morning coffee with my cat Zippy in my lap and re-watched Top Gun: Maverick. Later, I walked around my house and practiced my "Tell me about yourself" answer in preparation for upcoming interviews. I had an initial phone screen for a job that I decided not to pursue further. Later that afternoon, I drove to the location of the next day's interview and then picked up a few groceries on my way home. I spent about an hour lying on the floor in my office, staring at the ceiling. I slept fitfully that night and had nightmares about giving terrible answers to an unseen interviewer's horrible questions.

On **Friday** morning, I skipped grown-ups only roller skating to sleep in. I took my time getting ready for my job interview and arrived early. After 90 minutes of meetings with the hiring manager and one of my would-be future coworkers, I headed home. I canceled my plans to go to the board gaming group because my social battery was nearly dead. I looked at the basket full of clean clothes and realized hanging them up wasn't going to happen today either. I did a little yoga and went to bed early.

The Challenge of Getting Things Done

So far, you've had a chance to learn more about yourself, your work preferences, and your career goals. In addition, you now know a few basics about the financial, insurance, and healthcare decisions that need your attention right away. Understanding these core components is valuable when working through a significant life change. Fortunately, you are now armed with the knowledge you need to move forward.

Now comes the tricky part.

Even when you have a general idea of what needs to happen, sometimes it's hard to translate higher-level information into specific activities. Having a detailed list can help you take the right action to progress toward your goals. In this chapter, you'll find helpful week-by-week to-do lists to keep you on track. You can even customize them to ensure details specific to your situation are represented. It is much easier to do the right things when you have a list to guide you.

Now comes the even trickier part.

Even when you have a clear sense of your goals and a well-written to-do list (or three), another obstacle remains. Sometimes, even when you know what your top priorities should be and how urgent those tasks are, you still can't manage to get those crucial things done. How is that even possible?

In short, it all comes down to our energy. When life is puttering along as planned, we don't have to spend undue effort living our everyday lives. We know how to manage our jobs, spend time on our interests, and tend to our households. In more normal times, we expect the future to be a lot like the present, with a few small shifts. Like everyone, you may put off a few unpleasant or complex tasks here and there, but you usually have the capacity to contend with your regularly scheduled adulting.

Post-layoff, a lot has changed. Now, you are navigating uncharted territory, which can be exhausting. Losing your job upends your life and gives you a whole new set of problems you need to figure out how to solve. These problems also come with uncertainty about the future, new complexities in your financial life, and anxiety about how long it might take to get back to something that could be called normal. You are now entering an unplanned phase in your life where you will probably experience more rejection in a shorter period of time than ever before.

Some Days are More Difficult than Others

Some days will be amazing. Within a half hour of waking up, you receive an invitation to do a phone screen, notice another hiring manager accepted your LinkedIn connection request, and receive a message from a recruiter for a role that looks promising. Everything is going great for you. Hearing that good news fills you with hope. You feel appreciated, valued, and worthwhile. Soon, you're updating your budget, making that overdue phone call, and cleaning your whole kitchen. You use that extra burst of energy to start preparing for tomorrow's phone screen. Today, you are productivity personified.

Then there are the other days. You check your email and read, "We will not be moving forward with your application," then move on to "We regret to inform you," then finish up with, "This position is no longer available." You're not even out of bed, and you already heard you weren't good enough for three jobs you really wanted. All that good news from the previous day seems irrelevant. Your email is now a scary place where everyone is mean. You hop onto LinkedIn to look for new jobs. While looking at listings, you fixate on the one or two preferred qualifications you don't have. You start to customize a resume for one job, then stare at your screen, trying to figure out why anyone would bother hiring you.

You Are Not a Failure

After a three-rejection morning, you may feel like everything is hopeless. Despite how it feels right then, you are not lazy, a loser, or a failure. Instead, you have probably been going too hard for too long and have little to show for it yet.

In addition, you have probably been relying on the overly simplistic getting-things-done strategies people often bluster about. If your only plan for success involves hammering away, powering through, or pulling yourself up by your bootstraps, you will have problems. It's an excellent time to remind yourself that bucking/soldiering/cowboying up is not a long-term sustainable strategy. It is a short-term fix you can use occasionally when you have no other options. Making that once-in-a-while solution your go-to move will leave you irritable, burned out, and feeling like the failure you most certainly are not.

To find the right new job for you, even the best to-do list won't ensure success all by itself. You won't be able to push yourself beyond your limits consistently for very long. Given that many job searches last between a few weeks and several months, you will need to find a way to sustain your momentum over time.

Examine Your Energy to Manage Your Time

To position yourself for job search success, you need to identify the right actions for you to take to ensure you're making progress. You also need to figure out how to actually do those right things consistently with a more nuanced strategy than "I'll just tough it out."

Let's start with identifying what success looks like, listing out those right things to do, and exploring better ways to manage your time and energy.

Be a Realistic Optimist

Be sure to leverage your Realistic Optimist mindset by reminding yourself that good things are coming—as long as you put the work in to get there. While you can accomplish a lot, you'll never be able to do absolutely everything that may contribute to your success. Instead of setting unrealistic expectations for your ongoing productivity, you need to prioritize where you spend your energy and your time.

Sometimes, that means you'll go to an interview and later opt out of a fun event because your social battery is near dead. Other times, you'll stay home and watch a movie instead of going to another networking meet-and-greet because you prioritize your recovery over the possible connections you might make. This give and take will help you progress towards your goals without burning out.

What You Can and Can't Control

Before we talk about those right things to do and get to specific to-do lists, let's get crystal clear on a few more unpleasant realities of the situation. Like it or not, you cannot directly control the following job search variables:

- How long your career transition will last.
- When or if you'll get a phone screen, final interview, or job offer for a specific role.
- The length, content, and complexity of the interview process for a given job.
- Who else applies for the jobs you are pursuing, their qualifications, and who they might know.

However, here are the factors you can control:

- How many job applications you submit, and for which roles.
- How you respond to good or bad news about your job search.
- The quality and content of your LinkedIn profile, job application materials, and messaging.
- The relationships you cultivate within your professional network and how you ask for help.

Markers of Job Search Success

When we think about achieving a goal, we often focus on really big goals—like getting an awesome new job. However, it's not like you do one simple checkoffable activity and a big goal has been achieved. Big goals take weeks and months to complete. This type of big goal also only happens after you do many smaller tasks and a whole lot of things you can't control fall into line.

Leading and Lagging Indicators

Let's think through what success looks like during the job search in a tangible way.

An accepted job offer is one of the ultimate measures of job search success. This lagging indicator is a big goal that won't happen for a while and has many contributing factors.

This is where leading indicators come in. Leading indicators are all of the tasks you need to complete to position yourself to achieve that bigger goal. Leading indicators are those smaller, checkoffable things you can control.

Overall, you need to select, manage, and complete the right leading indicators to help you with your lagging indicator of getting a new job.

Leading Indicators of Job Search Success

Building on those things you can control, here are two specific areas you can control that will help contribute to you getting a new job:

- The number and quality of job applications you submit.
- The number of people you directly interact with in person and online.

Lagging Indicators of Job Search Success

Here are two specific lagging indicators of success. Remember, these are not entirely in your control. However, if you do enough of the right things consistently, you are more likely to experience these indicators:

- A hiring manager or recruiter contacts you to schedule an interview.
- An employer extends a job offer.

A Few Job Search To-Do Lists

When your emotions run high, it's easy to get overwhelmed. Having a list of tasks to complete helps battle inaction while keeping you focused on the right things. Use these as a starting point for writing lists that help you.

Your Week One To-Do List

Right after you have been laid off, immediate personal business needs to be addressed. You will need to focus your efforts here.

Get Your Head Right

- Pause and take time to process your emotions. Acknowledge the situation and work through it.
- As feelings arise, name the emotion and process each in a way that does not negatively impact your job search.
- Notify the people in your inner circle about your job status change. Look to them for support.
- Choose a Realistic Optimist mindset and filter your experiences through that lens.

Attend to Layoff Business

- Talk with members of your household about financial and insurance changes.
- List your career transition financial goals.
- Review and decide your next steps on any severance agreement you may receive from your former employer.
- Take necessary steps (consulting with a lawyer, asking for agreement modifications, signing a version of the agreement, or choosing not to sign) regarding any severance agreement with your former employer.
- Apply for Unemployment Insurance (UI) benefits in your state (if eligible).
- Consider other possible career transition income streams.

- Research and select the right options for paying for healthcare costs for your household.
- Consider fitting in trips to the doctor, dentist, or pharmacist while your current health insurance is still in effect.
- Take next steps regarding your option for paying for healthcare costs, which may include enrolling in your chosen health insurance option.
- Review your budget and scale back your expenses where possible.

Take Care of You

- Prioritize basic self-care.
- Acknowledge the progress you have made so far.
- After you complete your initial financial and insurance tasks, manage the emotions you may have after completing these milestone activities.
- Do at least one non-business, non-job searching activity that brings you joy.

Week One To-Don't List

- Don't start applying for all the jobs right away with no game plan.
- Don't freak out and take "any old job" out of sheer unbridled panic.
- Don't go full reality TV on social media and vomit your sadness, rage, and grief all over everyone.

Your Week Two To-Do List

After week one, you should have addressed the first wave of emotions and handled short-term financial and insurance concerns. Now, it's time to shift to job search prep.

Do Your Structured Soul Searching

- Set aside time to reflect on what you want to be when you grow up.
- Write a brief description of your longer-term career aspirations.
- Reflect on what you want to be next as you think about your next role.
- Identify and reflect on your values. Think about your hopes and what matters to you most.
- Identify and reflect on your talents and strengths. Think about which are most important to you.

Clarify The Details of What You Want in Your Next Job

- List your work-related preferences.
- List your target job titles.
- Identify your "must haves" and "nice to haves" in your new target job and prioritize each.
- Identify your overall salary needs and preferences.

Create Supporting Job Search Materials

- Assemble your work history.
- Assemble your educational and professional development history.
- Write your "What I Want" statement.
- Write your professional summary.
- Think through and write out your answers to frequently asked interview questions.
- Identify your target salary range and how it might change for different roles.

Create Job Application Materials

- Create your job-specific resume.
- Create your basic cover letter format.

- Gather and determine how to share your work samples with prospective employers.
- Identify your references and list their contact information.
- Contact your potential references and confirm their willingness to vouch for you.
- Determine how you will track your job search progress.
- Update your LinkedIn profile.

Take Care of You

- Prioritize basic self-care.
- Acknowledge the progress you have made so far.
- After preparing to launch your job search, manage the emotions you may have after completing these milestone activities.
- Connect with another member of your household or trusted person to help you when this process becomes overwhelming.
- Do at least one non-business, non-job searching activity that brings you joy.

Week Two To-Don't List

- Don't throw your hands in the air and say, "All this thinking is stupid," and just start applying for all the jobs right away with no game plan.
- Don't panic and take "any old job" just to have an employer again.
- Don't become disheartened and do absolutely nothing.
- Don't take to social media and tell anyone who will read it about the horrors of your job search and all of the companies, people, and whoever else is to blame.

The Fundamental Shift After Week Two

After the first two weeks of career transition, the reality of this significant life change may finally sink in. You may be painfully aware that your future is uncertain and feel lost. Your initial short-term worries will now change into bigger "I hope I don't screw up my whole life" fears.

This is a whole lot of hard-core adulting. During this job transition, you may work harder than ever, not have your usual paycheck, and feel like a failure due to your lack of meaningful results. It is emotionally taxing, exhausting, and just plain rough. You may also feel like people who have not been through this experience may not really get what you are going through or know how to help.

If you're doing great so far, I have two key insights. For one, good for you for being ridiculously resilient and getting the job done during a tough time. Secondly, realize that eventually, it will hit you like a freight train that you are going through one of life's most stressful transitions. The frenetic and fear-driven pace at which you powered through during weeks one and two is unsustainable.

In week three, you will transition from the quick flurry of getting it done to the realization that you have no idea how long this whole thing will last. You also may fall apart a little as you shift away from the do-it-all-right-now mentality. Now, it's time to transition to a longer-term view that involves you taking the right actions consistently to position yourself for job search success.

Week Three and Beyond To-Do List

In week three, we transition into regular job searching and life-living activities. Now, you'll see how daily and weekly to-do lists help you focus.

Your Daily To-Do List

This daily to-do list only includes one job search activity. Otherwise, these tasks are more about creating a little bit of normalcy and routine in your now predominantly unstructured days.

Morning	Afternoon	Evening
-Brush your teeth. -Shower. -Drink a glass of water. -Take your vitamins. -Clean your dishes. -Spend 1 hour on weekly to-do list tasks.	– Drink a glass of water. -Eat lunch. -Move for 30 minutes. -Go outside for 10 minutes. -Interact on LinkedIn for 30 minutes. -Spend 1 hour on weekly to-do list tasks.	-Drink a glass of water. -Eat dinner. -Plan the next day. -Stretch for 10 minutes. -Brush your teeth.

These tasks are small, checkoffable, and well within your control. They are also relatively simple. These are not SMART goals or stretch goals. Instead, this to-do list helps you care for yourself and feel like you accomplished at least something.

Your Weekly To-Do List

In addition to those daily tasks that help create a basic structure, here is a weekly to-do list to help you stay on track with activities to help your job search.

Keep Your Mind on Your Money

- Submit your weekly request for your unemployment payment.
- Review your budget. This may include checking your bank account balances, reviewing credit card activity, making sure bills are paid, and calling any creditors you might need to make other arrangements.

Job Searching

- Search for your target job titles using your favorite search engine or a site like LinkedIn or Indeed.
- Bookmark at least five jobs of interest
- Prioritize the jobs that interest you the most.
- For your first priority job, customize a resume and apply.

- For your second priority job, customize a resume and apply.
- For your third priority job, customize a resume and apply.
- Email thank you notes to each person who interviewed you this week.
- Send follow-up messages to any employers with whom you are waiting to hear back.
- Update your job search activity records.

Professional Networking

- Send five customized connection requests to people you'd like to have in your LinkedIn network.
- On LinkedIn, make a post sharing an article highlighting one of your professional skills.
- On LinkedIn, make a post sharing an inspirational quote.
- On LinkedIn, reshare a post originally made by one of your connections and include your comments.
- Attend a webinar or professional development meeting. Afterward, either invite at least one other attendee to connect on LinkedIn or create a LinkedIn post about what you learned.

Take Care of You

- Prioritize basic self-care.
- Acknowledge the progress you make each week.
- Address emotions as they come.
- Connect with another member of your household or a trusted person to help you when the process becomes overwhelming.
- Do at least one non-business, non-job searching activity that brings you joy.

Remember, the world doesn't end if you don't do all of these things, and you don't get a prize for doing more. For me, having these to-do lists helps me focus on doing the right things—even when I'm struggling.

All Hours are not Equally Productive

When I'm in a career transition, I spend a lot of time writing, applying for jobs, and interacting on LinkedIn. I also tend to rewatch TV shows and movies. Conventional time management would say that I'm wasting a good chunk of my life watching fictional people live theirs and that I should spend that time on the higher-value items on my to-do lists. In reality, it is not feasible to produce noteworthy results all the time. Achieving at a high level requires preparation and adequate recovery time. That means if I have two video interviews in one day, I will appear to be doing a lot of nothing for those couple of hours right afterward. The only way I can knock those interviews out of the park is by managing my energy well.

When I think of productivity as it compares to time, I think a lot about the time I spend writing as compared to the quality of my output. In some cases, I'll write for an hour and end up with a long, rambly nothing that I end up discarding. Other times, I write for an hour and create a valuable blog article or tidy up several book pages. So what's the difference? During the non-productive hour, I started with no real plan and wrote nothing valuable. Before my hyper-productive hour, I walked outside and let my mind wander. I devised an idea for a blog article, played with a few ways to organize it, and knew what I wanted to say before I sat down to type. This time around, my hour of writing flowed effortlessly.

Overall, it's not just about tallying up those hours and having a respectable number. Instead, work with your energy levels, balance planning and doing, and align your activities with your peak productivity times.

Reflect on Factors Influencing Your Energy Levels

As you think about how to spend your time, learn about yourself and when you will be the most productive and happiest with each activity. I interact with LinkedIn posts during my first cup of coffee, enjoy afternoon walks, and do yoga at night before bed. There are no absolute right or wrong times for most things, just ones that are a better fit for you.

Take time to reflect on your most and least productive times of day. Use these questions as a starting point:

- Are you a morning person, a night person, or somewhere in between?
- Are you an introvert, extravert, or somewhere in between?
- What time of day do you seem to get the most done?
- Do you think about something for a while before doing it, or do you jump right in?
- What tasks take you very little time? What tasks seem to take a long time?
- How much alone time do you need? How much social time do you need?
- How much structured time do you need? How much unstructured time do you need?

In addition, reflect on these factors and their impact on your energy levels:

- Working too long on the same task or switching between tasks too frequently?
- Too much or too little social contact?
- Too much or too little time at home?
- Having too many or too few new experiences? Having too much or too little routine?

Remember, there are no right or wrong answers, just what is true for you.

For me, I need social time, but I also need time to recover. I also need blocks of time to focus, reflect, and figure things out. I find it stressful when I switch between tasks frequently, and I try to balance my life between having new experiences and tried and true routines.

I also find that I need more familiarity when I am under stress (like during career transition). Since it is a time filled with so much change and rejection, I am more likely to spend more time sitting in my favorite chair and less time exploring new pastimes. Be sure to stay mindful of how you feel and use that information to figure out what you need right then.

Energy Builders

Now that you know what some of your energy depleters might be, let's look at ways to build your energy.

- **Basic self-care:** eating, drinking water, showering, moving your body, time outside, deep breathing, and stretching can help make you feel better almost immediately.
- **Accomplishing something:** sending an email, making a phone call, paying a bill, or wiping down your kitchen counters will help you feel like you made even the most minor contribution to the world today. There is something inherently satisfying about crossing a task off of your list.
- **Changing it up:** taking breaks, moving your body, going to a different grocery store, walking in a new place, driving a different route as you run errands, working from your kitchen table, or doing whatever you can to add newness to your daily routine.
- **Recovering:** sleeping, walking in nature, watching a movie you've seen before, reflecting on your day, playing games, journaling, and meditating, are all great ways to heal.

Prioritizing High-Value Job Search Activities

Plain and simple, there is not enough time to do everything you could possibly do. Therefore, it's crucial to prioritize your time. This helps make sure you are doing the highest value activities that get you closer to your goal of having the right day job for you. Know that saying yes to these higher-value activities means you'll have to say no to other things. In my case, I said no to a professional development meeting, a trip to the zoo, and roller skating because I prioritized job interviews and interview preparation. You'll need to protect your time to make space for what will help you the most. Here is my prioritized list of time-bound, high-value job search activities:

1. A job interview.
2. Job interview preparation.

3. Meeting with a professional colleague that may result in a job referral.
4. Attending a group meeting with professional colleagues where I'll have a chance to speak to the larger group and/or connect with individuals during or after the event.
5. Attending a webinar (where I don't get one-on-one interaction with people) on a topic that is interesting and useful to my job search.

Know, too, that your regularly scheduled routine will change when interviews pop up. Your comfortable morning routine may be preempted to prepare for tomorrow's interview, which you just learned about today. Having the ability to adapt your schedule based on opportunities is necessary.

Valuable Time and Energy Management Techniques

Here are a few more helpful time and energy management techniques.

Saying No

One of the best time management strategies is the simple act of saying no. When you're in between paid jobs, people may go out of their way to find ways to occupy "all that free time" you have. Being raised to be a nice, pleasant human being, I have a long history of saying yes to things I shouldn't have. While saying no can be difficult, in your role as the CEO of You, it's your job to prioritize your time wisely to help you achieve your goals.

You might want to say no to doing extra volunteer work for your local library, church, or favorite charitable cause. You might want to skip helping someone landscape their yard, paint their house, or move. You might want to avoid attending an additional school play, driving an extra carpool shift, or chaperoning one more event. In short, you get to spend your time in whatever activities bring you joy and/or get you closer to finding a new job. Ensure you align your time with your goals and do not take on additional tasks out of a sense of guilt, obligation, or good old-fashioned task avoidance.

Creating Your Schedule

One benefit of working for someone else (aside from the whole paycheck thing) is that it gives your life structure. When you're in career transition, making yourself some kind of schedule is valuable. It doesn't have to be rigid or rigorous. Having more structure is useful when you're struggling. Systems help because they give you some idea of what to do with yourself if and when your plans change. Even if you don't follow your schedule to the letter, having structure around your time can help address your need for order and give you a sense of accomplishment.

Planning for Alpha Work and Beta Work

Different types of work require different levels of energy. Based on a time management class I attended, tasks fall into two categories: Alpha and Beta work.

Alpha work requires a fair amount of brain power. Alpha work uses skills like critical thinking, prioritizing, and decision-making. Tasks like writing a blog article on phone screen interviews, building a class on creating your job search toolkit, or making a project plan as a work sample for a job application are all examples of Alpha work. This type of work is more complex and takes both contemplation and focus.

Beta work is more about doing. Beta work involves completing tasks like feeding the cats, taking out the garbage, and running a load of laundry. Usually, tasks are not difficult but just need to be done. Beta work can also be an excellent opportunity to do another fun activity, like listening to music or get a great idea on how to do other Alpha work you are considering.

When planning out your time, know that you may need more extended periods of uninterrupted time for Alpha work, and you may be able to fit in Beta work here and there. Be aware that you can't do Alpha work all the time. Be sure to mix it up to give your mind a rest so you have more success completing complex activities.

Blocking Off Time

If I have a blank calendar, I have difficulty accomplishing anything because I have too little structure. Conversely, if I overschedule myself, I will be frustrated because I have too much structure. Blocking off time for dedicated activities is how I balance the two extremes.

During these time blocks, which are usually one to two hours long (for me), I focus on the task at hand. For example, during this time, I might search for new open positions, customize my resume for a certain role, or write a few thank you messages. Making an appointment with myself helps me get things done.

I also block out time for fun activities. Whether when the roller skating rink is open, when my coffee group is meeting, or an hour to walk on a nice day, blocking off time helps me prioritize activities that bring me joy.

Batching Work

There are some things that I need to do multiple times in a day or a week or similar tasks that go well together. Work batching is a way to help increase your efficiency with these types of tasks. Here are a few examples of the kind of work I batch:

- **Searching for open positions:** I spend a half hour looking for jobs and bookmarking those that meet my basic requirements. If I'm not sure about a role, I'll bookmark it for now and review more later.
- **Prioritizing applications:** I spend a half hour reviewing my bookmarked jobs. Then, I read them more closely, eliminate the less desirable ones, and select which higher-value job applications I will submit.
- **Applying for jobs:** I start with my basic resume, review the job description, personalize the professional summary and skills sections of my resume, and then apply. I then update my status on my spreadsheet. I repeat this for the other jobs I will apply for in a given week.

Grouping tasks tends to improve efficiency and boost productivity.

Setting a Timer

Most people's productivity decreases the longer they work on the same task. One way to use your time more consciously is by using a timer. For example, I set a timer for 50 minutes, then take a 10-minute break. This way, I have a set time to focus, but I also know it won't last forever. In addition, if I'm spinning on a task and not accomplishing anything, taking that break usually gets me out of that thought trap.

During breaks, I switch gears. I stand up, stretch, or take a few deep breaths. Sometimes, I'll even do a quick Beta task, like folding towels, before returning to my Alpha work. When my timer goes off and my break ends, I begin again. Breaks can work wonders to stop you from spiraling by helping you re-engage with a given task.

You are the CEO of You

CEOs cannot say yes to everything. They need to say no to most things to focus on the items with the most significant impact. They cannot meet with everyone who requests a meeting or attend every in-person professional development meeting. They have to pick and choose to make the most of their time—and they don't apologize because prioritizing in this way empowers them to succeed.

You also need to prioritize your time and focus on those high-value activities. Remember, you're not saying no to all of those things, you are saying yes to you and what matters most as the CEO of You.

Lesson Summary

Post-layoff career transition can be one of the most challenging periods in life. You'll have less structure and less external validation and face more rejection than at any other time. After weeks one and two of career transition, it is necessary to focus not only on managing your time but also your energy.

Solid time management strategies are a good foundation for success. These include knowing your goals and understanding critical indicators of success. Now, you have a to-do list to help you accomplish essential tasks, from addressing initial financial concerns, paying for health care costs, and kicking off your job search well. You also have a week three and beyond to-do list to help you manage those right things you need to do to ensure job search success.

You also know the huge role that energy management plays. You're becoming mindful of your natural energy flow, what depletes you, and what builds your energy. You'll use what you learn to balance your job search priorities, work with your energy, and leverage fundamental time management techniques. You'll adjust your plans as needed and manage your time and energy to maintain productivity for however long your career transition may last.

Your Next Steps

- Revisit your short- and long-term job search goals.
- Make your own daily to-do list with activities to prioritize your self-care and create structure.
- Make your own weekly to-do list with activities to monitor your finances, keep your job search on track, and prioritize self-care.
- Reflect on factors influencing your energy levels.
- Identify energy builders that work for you.
- Incorporate what you learn into your daily and weekly to-do lists.
- Identify time management strategies you'll incorporate into your routine.

Lesson Seven: Assess, adapt, and rise above.

So Much for Plan A

After a challenging job search, I was overjoyed when I received an offer for a new Learning and Development Manager position. The hiring process had been a little all over the place, which is not uncommon for a startup, but now it was a done deal. I had negotiated and accepted the offer, and I was excited to get back to work. I breathed a sigh of relief, knowing that this period of unemployment would end in two short weeks.

I started to shift my mindset from job searcher to soon-to-be employed professional. The week after I formally accepted the job offer, I took down all indications of job searching on LinkedIn. While I didn't post my job title and employer name just yet, I shared a celebratory "Hooray, I got a job–more to come!" LinkedIn post. I planned a few fun non-job searching activities for the following week and started readjusting my sleep schedule back to office worker time.

A few days before my planned first day of work, I got a call from the recruiter letting me know that my agreed-upon start date was not going to happen. Apparently, the company had originally planned on this role starting in Q2, and now they wanted to hold off on my start date until they knew their Q1 sales numbers. While the new start date was still unknown, the recruiter estimated it should be within the next month and a half.

After multiple discussions with the recruiter and hiring manager, I left with renewed confidence that everything would work out. The hiring manager definitely wanted me for the role, and she had no concerns about the position still being a go. The only question was the actual start date, which she was sure she could resolve soon. I reiterated my plan to move forward with that job offer.

Two weeks after the date formerly known as my start date, I reached out to the hiring manager and then the recruiter for a progress update. A few days later, I received an email from the hiring manager with few details and no new start date. Again, I received assurances that I was the right person for the job. I still wanted to believe what they were saying about an impending start date.

A week or so later, I got the call from the recruiter saying that a start date would not be coming. Ever. The company was going in a different direction —one that did not involve me. Even during this conversation, the recruiter assured me that I was still the hiring manager's first choice—even though the role was now officially off the table. That was a hollow consolation prize.

You Will Hit Snags

When you're searching for a new job, there are always challenges. As you work through your process, you'll make new connections, apply for jobs, interact with people on LinkedIn, send follow-up messages, and interview. At least, that's how it's supposed to work. However, like with any system you put in place to solve a problem, it's helpful to compare the actions you've been taking to your results. Building this habit will help you identify how you might want to tweak your approach.

Let's revisit what success looks like in your job search so you can identify areas where you might need to assess, adapt, and rise above those roadblocks.

Be a Realistic Optimist

Throughout your job search, you'll get a lot of rejections. You won't get a phone screen after every application you submit. You won't get a follow-up interview for each first interview. You won't get an offer for every final interview you complete. Instead of thinking of those results as failures, consider them valuable insights into what is working and what isn't. Take rejections and use them to influence what you will start doing, stop doing, and keep doing in your job search. Know that if you keep doing the right things and focusing on what you can control, you will eventually achieve your goal.

Interview Progression Issues

After you apply for a job, your goal is to be selected for an interview. The whole hiring process usually includes an initial phone screen, one or more face-to-face interviews, and then a job offer. Let's look at possible places you might get stuck and how to evolve your approach.

Not Getting Phone Screens

I've seen variations on the following LinkedIn post way too many times: "I've applied for 300 jobs over the last six months, and I have only gotten a couple of interviews." Again, you won't get a phone screen for every job application you submit, but you should be getting some. If you apply for even 20 jobs and don't hear anything back from any of them, it's time to reassess and figure out what you need to change.

The first huge step in job searching is getting out of the virtual pile of applications and into the much more selective "We gotta talk to this one" pile. Taking these steps can help.

Step 1: Identify Your Target Job

Often, people who struggle with getting job interviews need to revisit what they want and focus their job search on that goal. Unfortunately, while applying for as many jobs as possible seems logical, it often backfires. Instead, job seekers who identify what they really want and apply for roles more closely matching their interests and qualifications get hired sooner.

Step 2: Revisit Alignment Between Goals and Job Search Messaging

Another problem shared by people who struggle is not emphasizing what they want, their work experience, and their most relevant qualifications. Ensure your resume has a strong Professional Summary highlighting the type of role desired and the value you bring.

Step 3: Focus on Fewer Applications

How many applications should you do in a given week? Applying for 300 jobs over six months (26 weeks) is an average of 11.5 applications per week. That is A LOT. When I'm job searching, my goal is three per week and as many as six if I see a few more roles that look promising. By focusing on fewer applications, I increase my quality instead of relying too heavily on quantity.

Step 4: Customize your Resume for Each Application

When I decide to apply, I take 15-30 minutes per application to customize my resume. Taking this extra time to update my language helps potential employers understand how my skill set aligns directly with what they are looking for in a candidate. Ensuring the right keywords are present for an Automated Tracking System (ATS) and for the recruiter who initially reviews resumes gives you a better chance of being selected. To make these updates efficiently and effectively, I focus on two sections: Professional Summary and Skills & Competencies.

Your Professional Summary

I use keywords included in the job posting to update my Professional Summary so it more closely aligns with their terminology.

For example, this is the first line in the Professional Summary for my general-purpose resume:

- Proactive learning and development leader driven to help individuals and organizations succeed.

Here are alternate statements reflecting the language in individual job postings:

- Entrepreneurial training manager who thrives when collaborating with stakeholders to design, develop, and deliver employee learning initiatives that drive results.
- Adaptable customer education lead who thrives when collaborating with subject matter experts to build client-facing learning and development programs that promote customer engagement.

I tailor my professional summary using language put together by the hiring organization. This makes it easier for the recruiter (who may not know much about the actual role) to see how I embody what they say they want in a candidate.

Your Skills and Competencies

I use the Skills and Competencies section as another opportunity to use the hiring organization's language. For example, I include the general industry keywords "coaching" and "eLearning" in my all-purpose resume. When I tailor my resume for a specific role, I use their words. "Coaching" becomes performance coaching, employee coaching, or providing constructive feedback; "eLearning" becomes on-demand e-learning, online learning, or interactive online courses.

Again, by fine-tuning my wording to align with their job posting, I am making sure I speak the same language as the company evaluating my skills.

Not Getting Face-to-Face Interviews

If you're not moving on to second interviews, it's time to up your phone screen game. Performing well during your first interaction with a hiring manager or recruiter will give you a better chance of being invited to the next phase in the process. Taking these steps can help.

Step 1: Anticipate Interview Questions

As a reminder, here are common phone screen questions:

- Tell me about yourself.
- Why are you looking for a new job?
- Why are you interested in this role?
- What do you know about our company?
- What is your desired salary?
- What questions do you have for me?

Remember to tailor your answers for the specific job and employer.

Step 2: Research the Role

- **Review the job posting.** Refamiliarize yourself with the job title, core responsibilities, purview, and desired qualifications for this role.
- **Investigate further.** Use your favorite search engine to look up unfamiliar acronyms and figure out how to relate your experience and qualifications to their needs. Be ready to speak in the words they use in the job posting and relate your work stories to that job.
- **Skim your resume.** Since you applied with a customized resume, reacquaint yourself with how you described your skills. Determine how you will use the points you include in the stories you'll tell to answer behavioral interview questions.

Step 3: Research the Company and Your Interviewer

- **Check out the company on LinkedIn.** Note the industry they are in, what their products and services are, their size, headquarters location, and their recent posts. If you haven't done so already, follow their company page. Bonus points for interacting with their posts.

- **Visit the company's website.** Take a look at their mission, vision, and values. See what press releases are on their site and any awards they may have received. Look at their marketing materials. Review information on their leaders. Consider signing up for their newsletter.
- **View your interviewer's LinkedIn profile.** Note the schools they attended, where they live, their work history, mutual connections, and their recent posts. Find out what you have in common so you can have an engaging conversation. Consider following your interviewer on LinkedIn.
- **Reach out to connections.** If you know anyone who is a current or recent employee, ask them about their first-hand experience at the company.

Step 4: Write Out Answers to Common Interview Questions

Now, back to those questions. If you're not getting second interviews, examine your answers. Instead of just practicing them aloud, write them out. Make sure your responses are clear and concise. Writing each word out and then deciding what to include and what to cut will help you optimize your answers.

Step 5: Practice Your Answers Out Loud

Look in the mirror and answer each question. Have a phone call with a friend or former coworker and practice. Ask for feedback. Make sure you sound practiced but not canned. Strive to sound genuine, positive, and interested in the role. It's not just the words you say but the energy you convey to the interviewer.

Not Getting Offers

First off, take a moment to celebrate your successes. You are getting interviews! You are doing a whole bunch of things right! Now, it's time to revisit the content you're sharing with potential employers, how you structure answers to questions, and how you connect with individual interviewers. Taking these steps can help.

Step 1: Reflect on Your Previous Interview Performance

Think about your previous interviews. What went well? Where could you have done better? What question stumped you? Were you nervous?Improve your interview prep to ensure you incorporate your lessons learned and continuously improve.

Step 2: Review Your Stories

In most interviews, you'll talk about your skills through stories as you answer behavioral interview questions. To create clear and concise answers, remember to use a method to structure your answers. This might be CARL (Challenge, Action, Results, Learning) or another method that works for you. Be ready with a story to showcase your relevant skills. This will also limit rambling.

Step 3: Practice People Skills

Part of your success in a job interview (in addition to having the right skills and presenting yourself well) is being likable. Since people like to work with people who they like and respect, your ability to connect with your interviewers will be a great help. Write down and use the names of your interviewers. If you're unsure how to pronounce someone's name, ask them to pronounce it so you can use it correctly. Notice topics that people discuss and add your information on that same topic. Again, learn about interviewers by reviewing their LinkedIn profiles so you have a head start on possible topics of conversation.

As needed, practice having conversations with friends and former colleagues. Ask for their feedback and incorporate their suggestions.

Additional Job Search Challenges

Even when you have good results with your overall job search and hear back from companies on specific roles, you'll still face obstacles. Let's look at a few of those challenges.

Not Being Selected to Interview for "The Perfect Job"

Sometimes, you will find the perfect job. It's got a great title, a salary range above what you were thinking of asking, and you have a unique skill set that would make you exceptional in this position. Before applying, you dream about how fantastic your first day will be. You think to yourself, "This is the one!"

Unfortunately, you may not even get as much as an initial phone screen for this position—even when you feel like the job was tailor-made for you.

Possible Reasons Why

- **The position may not actually be open.** It may be an old listing, the role is on hold, they are gauging interest (and not hiring), there is an internal candidate, or it may already be filled.
- **You may not be as qualified as other applicants.** There's always the chance that someone somewhere has a better skillset than you—or their resume is more optimized and catches the recruiter or hiring manager's attention. It happens.
- **There may be a lot of applicants.** Especially for remote roles, there may

be hundreds of applicants, and companies only interview a handful of people. If an employer phone screens 10 of the 500 applicants, that means you had a 98% chance of not getting a phone screen.

Strategies to Adapt

- **Gather first-hand information from people in your professional network.** This may help you tailor your application materials even better than general online research.
- **When possible, get a referral.** Getting someone within the company to recommend you for a role often helps. They may even be able to get your resume in front of the hiring manager with an encouraging "This person is amazing. Check them out!" Remember, though, you still have to be well-qualified.
- **Customize your resume for each role.** Anything you can do to make it easier for the recruiter to see that your skills are indeed the skills needed for the job helps.
- **Apply for multiple jobs with different employers.** A company somewhere has the right job for you. Maybe this one just isn't it.

You May Fall in Love with a Job—"Your Job"

Inevitably, as a job searcher, you run across it. It's not just THE job, you also start thinking of it as YOUR job. It's the one you know in your heart is meant to be yours. It's perfect—easy commute, a great title, your dream company, and the job description lists the exact things you want to do. You think to yourself, "Why should I even bother applying for anything else because this is so my job!"

How It Feels

As you interview for it, during each interview, you feel more and more like this will be the one. You really connect with your possible boss. You love hearing about their annual conference, their fun chat thread that is nothing but pets, and how they thoughtfully assign people to work on projects that leverage their strengths. They keep asking you to progress to the next step in the interview process. This is totally YOUR job!

Except, well, it's not actually your job yet. You have made the mistake of falling in love with a job. You stop applying for other roles and even think about canceling a phone screen with another company because you're just certain an offer is inevitable. You're already picking out your outfit for your first day and thinking about how you'll tell everyone about the job you will be starting soon—which is also the best job ever!

As hard as it is to hear when things seem to be going well, in the misquote by Yogi Berra (and the infamous words of Lenny Kravitz), it ain't over 'til it's over. No matter how much they say they like you, indicate you would be perfect for the role, or say they can't imagine anyone else in the position, it's not your job yet.

When you receive a formal written offer, finish negotiating, and sign your offer letter, it is (in most cases) your job. It is for real and for true your job when you finish your first day of work.

Until then, no matter how excited you are, it is still only a promising job prospect.

Strategies to Adapt

- **Any time you fall in love with a job or think of it as "your job," make an extra effort to apply for additional openings.** If the job you see yourself in works out, great. If not, you're still working towards your ultimate goal of finding a new role complete with a paycheck—and you haven't lost days and weeks on something that did not come to pass.
- **Understand there is no perfect job.** However, there are a lot of good jobs that will be a solid fit for you and your skill set. Keep progressing towards your ultimate goal of finding a paying job that meets your requirements—which may or may not be this one.
- **Job descriptions can also be a little all over the place.** You really don't know what this job is from the written job description alone. You'll

learn a lot between reading the initial posting and interacting with interviewers. You might discover this one is great or isn't what you hoped.

- **Be sure to objectively evaluate the company, not just look for the positives.** Don't decide something is perfect and overlook the warning signs. Continue to keep an open mind as you learn more about an open role and the organization.

Assessments and Job-Specific Work Samples

Depending on the company, the newness of the position, and the level of the role, there may be more to the interview process than talking with all the stakeholders.

Potential employers may also ask you to complete projects to demonstrate the skill set you told them about in your resume. Some may rely on your portfolio and samples of your previous work. Others may want you to complete work samples as a part of the interview process. This could take the form of assessments or completing unpaid work to demonstrate your skills.

My Assessments

As a part of a few hiring processes, I've been asked to take various tests to assess my tendencies, abilities, and aptitudes. Focus areas often include problem-solving, strengths, work style, spatial ability, logical thinking, and temperament.

For one role after layoff number seven, the first two "interviews" with one organization were online assessments that compared my test results to a role-specific ideal profile. For that job opening, I had two "interviews" like this and received a rejection email without interacting with an actual human. For another hiring process, I took online exams on logical reasoning, general intelligence, and basic math before I was eligible for a phone screen.

In some cases, assessments may be included later in the process to gather supplemental information right before making an offer.

My Job-Specific Work Samples

As I've progressed into higher-level roles, projects have become more elaborate. Here are a few examples:

- For a manager role, I completed a 30-60-90 day onboarding plan for myself. For that same role, I also listed what equipment, software, and other resources I would need to begin creating videos for the company.
- For a consultant role, I was tasked with creating an innovative solution for employee onboarding for new contractors and full-time employees. For this project, I designed a pitch deck to garner buy-in from stakeholders. I delivered that presentation to a group including the hiring manager, other managers, and team members. In addition, I designed a blended learning solution that leveraged subject matter presenters and accommodated people having different locations and start dates.
- For a program manager role, I was tasked with creating an innovative onboarding program to teach new full-time staff about company products. I designed a new hire career fair showcasing different products, complete with a passport for trainees to collect stamps. Those trainees who visited each table and filled out their passports were enrolled in a prize drawing for a bigger company-branded prize.
- For a director role, during the initial application, I answered several essay questions and submitted a resume and a cover letter. Later in the process, after taking two professional assessments, I was also tasked with three more projects.
- For another director role, I signed a non-disclosure agreement and was asked to design a section of a course for one of their current clients. Then I completed their "in-box experience," which included "working" (to be clear, unpaid working) in their office for a half day and even presenting the solution to a client.

Ultimately, I did not receive job offers for any of these roles. It also felt varying degrees of icky to be tasked with hours of unpaid, highly skilled work that provided value for a company. I was also out 2-45 hours of time and trouble and received compliments on my work but no compensation (or job offer) for my time and trouble.

In the abstract, I've seen many people bluster on social media about what they won't do as part of an interview process. I also don't necessarily disagree with the boundaries those people suggest. I do know that making that decision feels much different in the throes of job searching. When asked to do a few projects to help you get a job you think you'll love, it's often hard to say no. Here are a few suggestions for deciding what you are willing to do during the interview process.

Strategies to Adapt

- **Decide in advance how much time you are willing to spend completing projects.** For example, would you be okay with one, two, or five hours of unpaid project work to demonstrate your skills?Determine the maximum hours of work you are willing to do before you are in front of a potential employer. This will help you make a better decision when the situation arises. Only you can decide how much uncompensated work you're willing to do for any given opportunity.
- **Think about how you might communicate your boundaries during the interview process.** You might commit to a specific number of hours, offer to do paid work for a reduced hourly rate, or decide to withdraw.
- **Be ready to assess the projected workload against your interest and likelihood of getting the job.** You may need to revisit your previously made decision at the time the work is presented. As you are closer to the final stage in the hiring process, you may be more willing to participate in a project. Know that your decision on what or how much to do will vary with each opportunity.

The Process is All Over the Place

The job interview process can be anything from one interview to many, many interviews depending on the organization and the role. Usually, you can expect some kind of logical progression, including the following: recruiter phone screen, hiring manager interview, VP interview, interview with possible coworkers, and offer. Sometimes–not so much.

How It Might Look

Some companies will have a pre-defined, structured process for the pacing and format of interviews, even including a standard list of questions for use at every stage. Other organizations will appear to be making it up as they go along. You may inadvertently skip steps and realize near the end that you missed discussing a basic topic like salary range or work location. You may have multiple one-on-one interviews with several people, including a recruiter, the hiring manager, coworkers, possible collaborators, human resources, and executives. Sometimes, the interview process may seem never-ending because you have not yet talked with everyone in the organization.

Know, too, that most people involved in the hiring process probably don't hire much. In addition, they also have "day jobs" and business goals they need to achieve. Consequently, they may tell you in one interview that they were working to hire someone "yesterday," then take what feels like forever after your interview to let you know about the next steps. At once, they both desperately need to fill their open positions and will put hiring on the back burner when they are busy putting out fires. These same people, who took extra days or even weeks to get back to you, may also want you to start as soon as possible once you have accepted an offer.

Strategies to Adapt

- **Ask about their hiring process.** This way, you at least know what the process should look like and how long it may take from start to finish. This will help you manage your expectations.

- **Apply for multiple positions at different employers.** They won't all be equally terrible.
- **Decide when you're no longer interested in a company.** When you reach the point when you've had enough, consider withdrawing from the position. You get to decide when it's no longer worth it for you.

Having a Job Offer Rescinded

Hooray! You have a new job! Finally, after what feels like a long, drawn-out period of unemployment, you have accepted a job offer–and you start in two weeks! However, there is always the outside chance that the job offer won't result in you working at that company. Personally, it has only happened to me once in my career, but when it does happen, it stings A LOT.

How It Feels

This is one of those cases where your thoughts and feelings sort of gang up on you all at once. During the gap between an accepted offer and a start date, you might feel guilty for doubting the job would come through. Once a job offer evaporates, you may feel angry for not getting wise to the reality of the situation a little earlier. You may be kicking yourself for stopping looking for jobs and making premature LinkedIn profile updates. You may feel like an idiot for only doing half-hearted "just in case" job-searching activity during the ambiguous lag time.

Strategies to Adapt

- **Rethink your standard operating procedure for what to do when you receive a job offer.** I suggest keeping your social media accounts in job-searching mode until you start your new role. During that time, especially an extended wait, continue to talk to other companies, apply for additional positions, and interview. Then, after you work at least a day and as long as a week at your new job, announce your new role.

- **When accepting a job, consider your next steps if the offer falls through.** The act of thinking through that possibility will help ease your anxiety.
- **When the conditions of the job offer change, reassess.** When changes to your start date or any aspect of the job offer become apparent, evaluate that information alongside other data you have about the role and projected start date. Make your decisions accordingly.
- **If your job offer is rescinded, take time to feel your feelings before moving forward.** If you don't process your emotions, they will come out sideways at just the wrong moment. Take time for self-care.
- **Plot, scheme, and relaunch your search.** If you find yourself in a position where you have announced your new role and the offer is rescinded, formally restart your job search. Begin with a new LinkedIn announcement stating that the position you previously accepted is no longer in play. Then, ask for assistance in finding a new role. Return to your previous plan of doing those right things to work towards your goal of new paid work.

Your Evolving Job Requirements

Earlier, we discussed the value of knowing what you want, what you don't want, and what would be okay. As your job search continues longer than you initially hoped, you'll readjust your thinking on what is acceptable for you in your next role.

Your Acceptable Job May Change Over Time

When you put together your target job, it is just that: your target. As you compare your target job to the market, you will need to revisit your priorities. Know that one factor that may influence the type of job you take will be the time you spend in the job market. Here is how that transition might look:

- **In months one and two** of your job search, you may be stringent about the characteristics of the job you will accept. You may be set on getting your dream title, at your dream salary, with your dream benefits, and working 100% remote.
- **In months three and four,** you may ease your requirements based on the responses you've been getting from employers. At that point, you may be open to a really good title, or even an okay title, okay benefits, and even an okay or acceptable salary. However, 100% remote may be non-negotiable for you.
- **During months four, five, and six,** when you know the end date for your unemployment payments is drawing near, you may stumble across a job with a more junior title but with a really good salary really good benefits that is hybrid with only occasional onsite work needed. This might be the right combination for you.
- **After six months**, you may be in a position where you need to start earning income since your unemployment payments are over. Now, you may be most concerned about a really good salary, be okay with no benefits (because maybe you're on another household member's plan), and take a 100% remote contract gig with a solid hourly wage.

You are the CEO of You

At the end of the day, remember your role as the CEO of you and make a decision that aligns with your overall career and life goals. If you are committed to getting a job meeting all of your requirements, know that it may take a little longer to find that job. Know, too, that you get to hold out for that job. Also, know that it's okay to adjust what you want based on your current situation. Do what makes the most sense for you and your household.

Lesson Summary

Throughout your career transition, pause intermittently, evaluate what you're doing (and how well it's working), and adjust your approach when needed. Instead of applying for hundreds of jobs and getting no response, you'll apply for jobs for a couple of weeks, then adjust your approach as needed, you'll look at where you hit some snags in the interview process–whether that's at the phone screen, interview, or offer level–and modify your approach to ensure additional job search success.

You also have a greater awareness of the confounding factors that might make your job search more challenging. You also understand that not every job will be right for you. You'll keep doing the right things, adjust your approach as needed, learn, adapt, and overcome.

Remember, you get to change your mind on what makes the most sense for you. Your thoughts on what you need in a job will evolve as you learn more. Remember, you get to decide what makes the most sense for you. As the CEO of you, make the best business decision to advocate for yourself and get what you need from your next paid position.

Your Next Steps

- Commit to reviewing your job search progress regularly.
- Use steps to address your job search issues to evolve your approach.
- Think about possible job search issues and how you plan to handle them beforehand.
- Determine the factors influencing your contingency plans and identify courses of action that work for you

The Long Awaited Happy Ending

Nine Months in the Making

After layoff number seven, I weathered a nine-month-long job search. During this time, I applied for 159 jobs, had 56 interviews, met with 28 different companies, participated in four final interviews, received two job offers, and had one offer rescinded.

I had six job interviews for one role before they decided to pursue other candidates. I met with eight recruiters who reached out to me, then saw five of them fall off the face of the earth after what I thought were promising conversations. I spent two weeks overfocusing on one role that didn't pan out, a month waiting for a job start date that never came, and an excruciating 90 days between Thanksgiving and the first full week in January convinced that I'd never work again.

Fortunately, after a tumultuous 264 days, I also landed somewhere wonderful.

I am excited to be able to leverage my strengths at a company that aligns with my values. I'm in a role where I both lead and get to be an individual contributor. It's a small company where I get to take organizational development programs to the next level. I work on a tight-knit team with talented people who care about what they do, are committed to ongoing improvement, and focus on helping the organization grow and develop. I'm happy with how the job aligns with who I am and where I want to be professionally. I feel like I found the right role for me.

Along the way, I identified and documented these lessons learned.

Lesson One: Experience your emotions and manage your mindset.

Right after a layoff, people often think about everything they have to do–all the while wrestling with shock, fear, anger, sadness, and shame. While you may feel compelled to take extreme action immediately, remember that you will not make your best decisions when in a highly emotional state. Before you spring into motion, feel your feelings and get your head on straight.

Take the time to address all of those feelings and work through them. You need to grieve the loss of routine, be angry about your job ending, and be afraid of what your unknowable future might hold. You also need to continue to assess and address all of the feelings that will crop up along the way. Build in the process of experiencing your emotions throughout your career transition. If you don't acknowledge and work through the emotions that crop up, you will struggle more with your career transition. Those unresolved feelings may come out sideways as rage, resentment, and blaming at just the wrong times.

In addition to experiencing your emotions, you also need to manage your mindset actively. In your newly claimed role as the CEO of You, treat your job search as your business. Make sound choices, keeping your wants, needs, and goals in mind. Remember your Realistic Optimist mindset as you navigate your job search. Staying realistic about job search challenges will help you make more effective plans for the situations you will face. Remaining optimistic about people's willingness to help and the good things the future holds will help you make it through the ups and downs of your career transition.

Lesson Two: Keep your mind on your money (and your money on your mind).

Within the first week of your layoff day, assessing your finances and working through necessary financial business is mission critical. Even if you aren't someone who enjoys managing your money, keeping a close eye on your money will help ease your anxiety during this time of transition.

Start by setting your short-term financial goals, usually some version of "lights on, doors open," to get you from your final payment from your previous employer to your first paycheck from a new job. Using a 6-12 month planning time horizon should help you consider how to address a longer-than-expected job search. Think through your short-term goals, like consistently paying your main bills, and longer-term goals, like a significant purchase. As you address challenges during your career transition, don't create problems for your future self that you'll have to dig out of later on.

Early on, apply for unemployment insurance (UI) benefits if you are eligible. Remember, this interim income stream is there to help you transition from your former job to your future job with as few bumps and bruises as possible. Take a look at your expenses and minimize or eliminate any expenditures that are not essential at this time. Explore options for paying for healthcare costs, do your research, and make the decision that is best for your household. Even through the challenges, be sure to find joy along the way.

Lesson Three: Ask yourself, "What do you want to be next?"

Few people take the time to step back from their work life and think, "Is this really what I want to do?" When you go through a layoff, you have an amazing opportunity to revisit what exactly you want from work.

Think about the values that you hold dear. Explore your strengths and talents to identify them and determine how to leverage those skills going forward. Take the time to think about what you've liked and disliked in previous jobs. Chat with your former coworkers and ask them about their first-hand impressions of working with you.

Put together a list of what you want from your next role. Think about the hours you want to work, the tasks you'd like to do, the ones you would love to never have to do again, and even your specific working arrangements. Think about the salary and benefits and which components matter the most to you. Think about the job titles, company types, and responsibilities you'd love to have. Get specific about what you really want, what you'd be okay with, and what is a straight-up no for you.

Lesson Four: Shape and share your story.

Finding a new job is all about telling the story of your career. Take the time to gather details about your previous work experience, then use that information to create your job search toolkit to help you share your story. Create your job search messaging, LinkedIn profile, resume, cover letter, work samples, and references so you're ready to tell the different parts of your career story to potential employers.

Use those materials about your story to tell potential employers more about your relevant skills. Using the text in job postings and information you gather from company and role research, you'll shape your story to show how your skill will be an asset to their organization.

Using these same techniques, you can use content from your resume and LinkedIn profile and information from the employer to create the answers to typical interview questions. Leverage best practices for answering interview questions to connect with the hiring team and the organization. Then, use the CARL method to tell a clear and compelling story of the context, action, result, and learning from your previous experience and illustrate your transferable skills.

Lesson Five: Help people help you.

Even if you want to do everything yourself, now is the time you need to ask for help. As you do that, make sure you're helping people to help you. By understanding what you need and the skill sets of specific people, you can more impactfully act for the kind of assistance you need.

Start by building your career support team. Think of who might be able to help you with emotional support, communication, logistical support, accountability, and just plain fun. In the professional realm, find those people who can share their professional insight or introduce you to others who might be able to point you in the right direction.

As you strive to deepen your professional relationships with new and existing connections, learn how to leverage LinkedIn. Make sure you build mutually beneficial relationships with colleagues. In addition, when asking individuals for help, tailor the type of ask to the state of your relationship. Make small, strategic asks, and be sure to help others as you ask for help along the way.

Lesson Six: Examine your energy to take control of your time.

When it comes to time management, it's not quite as easy as one might think. It's part knowing what to do and part figuring out how to make that happen when many aspects of life might feel like a struggle. Having the right combination of overarching goals, markers of success, task lists, and coping strategies will help you make much-needed progress–and give yourself a break on your less productive days.

From a time management perspective, you now have a good starter lists of what success looks like at different times during your career transition. Adjust those as needed for what makes the most sense for you. In addition, you now have a better initial grasp of things in and outside your direct control. Remember to control what you can–like how many job applications you submit, the timeliness of your follow-up messages, and the company research you do to tailor applications for each role.

On the energy management front, now you have a better idea of your energy levels and a few coping strategies for working with your energy to get the right things done. I also hope you have enough self-compassion to not beat yourself up for not always being a super achiever. Above all, be kind to yourself and celebrate your successes.

Lesson Seven: Assess, adapt, and rise above.

In general, through this book, you probably have a pretty good idea of what those right things are to do during your job search. A lot of job searching is doing those right things consistently over time, knowing that you'll make progress. In addition to doing those right things consistently, it's also valuable to reflect regularly to make adjustments as needed.

Looking at your results to date and reviewing trends is an integral part of the process. Look at where you're getting stuck and see what you might need to change. Look for how you tend to get stuck and how to change your approach. For example, depending on how you are progressing through the interview process at multiple companies, you may need to tweak your resume, prepare differently for interview questions, or modify how and when you reach out to people during your job application process.

In addition, it can be helpful to think through possible situations you may encounter. Taking the time to think through when you might want to withdraw from an interview process, saying no to submitting what you consider excessive work samples, or determining when a company is not right for you can help you progress toward a job that will be a good fit for you. You can also think about what is most important to you in a new role and how that might change based on what you learn about yourself along the way and the length of your unemployment. Remember, as the CEO of You, you get to decide how and when to adjust course to make the best business decision for you.

A Few Parting Thoughts

Have I seen my final layoff? I hope so. Regardless, there's no way to know what exactly the future will bring. I know I am committed to doing well in my current role while continuing to develop my skills, build my professional network, and plan for possible contingencies so I'm ready for whatever life throws at me.

I do know that I am happy to feel like I've found the right role for me that is aligned for where I'm at and where I want to be.

Here is my overall message of hope for you. Above all, keep in mind that you will get through this. Like the literally millions of people who have weathered a career transition, know that you'll be okay. Commit yourself to doing those right things consistently, and keep on keeping on. Your long-awaited happy ending is coming, too.

About The Author

Brenda L. Peterson knows her way around a layoff. Since forever, Brenda has worked in the field of learning and development—except for the many, many times she's had her position eliminated. All told, Brenda has had seven workdays that started with lots of obligations, but ended in unemployment. Now, Brenda shares her lessons learned at **TheLayoffLady.com** where she waxes poetic on layoffs, job transitions, and career resilience.